MJ/
//

C40

FUNN

"A
the
aut
she
Teen
the h
feelin
the wr
lilt and
here is

rare historic account of Protestant childhood life during
troubles, full of spirit, courage and humour. It is also an
autobiography by a survivor of child abuse who makes clear
refuses to be defined or limited by that experience.
...agers and adults can read this book knowing they are in
...nds of a born narrator who they can trust with their
...es. There is nothing either gratuitous or sentimental in
...ling. The book and the author sing with a true Irish
...d sparkle. For those who remember Cider in the fire,
...he modern classic in the making." Dr Valerie Sinason.

Funny Peculiar

CONSTANCE McCULLAGH

BRANDON

A Brandon Original Paperback

First published in Britain and Ireland in 2008 by Brandon
an imprint of Mount Eagle Publications
Dingle, Co. Kerry, Ireland, and
Unit 3, Olympia Trading Estate, Coburg Road, London N22 6TZ, England

www.brandonbooks.com

Copyright © Constance McCullagh 2008

The author has asserted her moral rights

ISBN 978-086322-384-6

2 4 6 8 10 9 7 5 3 1

Cover design: Anú Design
Typesetting by Red Barn Publishing, Skeagh, Skibbereen
Printed in the UK

To my mum, for giving me my love for life,
and to Rachel, for everything.

So it is better to speak
remembering
we were never meant to survive.

Audre Lorde, "A Litany for Survival"

Foreword

THIS BOOK TELLS the true story of my childhood from the age of four to fourteen. Although my brother and sister feature in the telling, this is not their story. I have, for reasons of privacy, changed their names and the names of other characters in the book. The events described are true but I have, on occasion, compressed them or changed the timeframe for structural reasons.

I would like to thank Steve MacDonogh of Brandon Books for having faith in *Funny Peculiar* and giving me the chance to tell my story. Despite the recent rash of "misery memoirs" there is still a great deal of secrecy associated with sexual abuse in the family and little understanding of how a child can survive such abuse and still retain a capacity for love and life.

I have been supported by a number of people in coming to terms with what happened to me. I would particularly like to thank Rachel Wingfield, Emerald Davis, Julie Bindel, Liz Kelly, Helen Morales and Kate Cook. I would also like to thank everyone who encouraged me in the writing of this book, especially Alyson Campbell, Anna Feuchtwang, Denise Marshall, Anne Wingfield and the Lauderdale House writing group.

I would like to acknowledge the vital role of the women's movement in creating the space for women (and men) like me to speak out about sexual violence and in providing much needed services for survivors. In particular I'd like to honour the memory of Andrea Dworkin, who fought so hard against the abuse of women and children and whose personal support I will never forget.

And finally I would like to thank all those survivors whose courage has helped to inspire me to fight back.

Prologue

A Little Forgetful

IT WAS A Saturday morning, April 1989. I was travelling by train from Winchester to Bristol when I realised I'd forgotten something important. Not my undies, wallet or house keys—these I had checked before leaving the house. No, the important thing I'd forgotten was the fact that I'd been sexually abused as a child. It seems a strange thing to have forgotten, I admit it. More than a little remiss. But then I suppose I've always been a little forgetful.

I was four when it started. I don't remember the exact date—somewhere in July 1970. It was a sunny summer's day, and I played in the garden in the bath. It was a cream plastic bath, about 2½ feet long and 6 inches deep. My mother would fill it with water and carry it out to the back garden where I would play happily for hours.

Someone had bought me a tea set for Christmas. It had a teapot, milk jug, cups, saucers and plates, all in red and white plastic. I was disappointed at the time—I'd been hoping for some toy cars. I hated playing tea parties. Ignored for months, it lay at the back of the cupboard until it was resurrected for the bath. I would fill the teapot with the bath water and then pour it from cup to cup, counting the number filled. Variations on this theme could absorb me for hours.

That particular day I was pretending I was at the beach. We lived in Coleraine, five miles from the Antrim coast, and I loved to go to the beach, even though I couldn't swim properly yet. I would splash around in the sea, kicking up great sprays of water. Or I'd sit near the shore and feel the tide pulling against me as the waves sucked back and forth. If my dad was in a good mood he'd bring the airbed. My brother, sister and I would clamber on behind him, and he'd paddle out to where the bigger waves would crash against us, sometimes toppling us off the airbed or surfing us into shore.

My brother and sister were already at the beach that day. Mrs O'Brien from next door had taken them with her kids who were the same age. They all squeezed into her beaten-up Beetle. I was younger and they said there wasn't enough room.

I cried to my mother when they went. "I wanted to go, too. The beach is my favourite. Why do I always have to be the youngest? I'm sick of it. Now I'm all on my own."

"Let's pretend we're at the beach, too," she said. "I'll fill the bath with water for you to play in, and I'll bring out a deckchair and sunbathe for an hour."

So while I rushed off to change into my ruffled blue bathing costume, my mother got out the old cream bath, filled it with cold water and carried it out to the back garden. She even put a bit of salt in it to make it taste more like the sea.

Soon I was absorbed in my water games, sailing saucers the length of the bath, loaded down with precious cargoes; leaves and sticks from the garden had turned into the treasures of the world. I'd seen the ships unloading at the harbour in Coleraine, and I used my arm as a crane, swinging it over the edge of the bath, stretching my hand wide and snapping it shut above the cargo. Then slowly I'd swing it back to dry land and deposit the leaves on the plates.

All afternoon I played, stopping only for drinks of orange juice, not objecting when my mother went off to do some baking. Late in the afternoon she called me indoors for a slice of fresh apple tart. It was still warm and she let me have some ice cream on the side as an extra treat.

I was still in the kitchen eating when my dad got home early from work. I heard him talking to my mother in the hallway.

"Where are the kids? I thought I'd take them to the beach for a swim before tea."

"Pat took the other two after lunch. But I'm sure Constance would love to go. She's been out there on her own all afternoon, God love her."

I expected him to say no, that it wasn't worth the bother for just me. But then my mother came into the kitchen and said, "Eat that up. Your dad's going to take you to the beach."

I gobbled the rest of my tart down, then went to the toilet while my mother put my clothes and a towel into a bag.

Soon we were off to Castlerock, the nearest beach, me sitting in the front in my mother's seat. I was excited but I didn't chatter on to my dad. It would only put him in a bad mood, and that would mean less time at the beach.

We parked behind the sand dunes. My dad opened the boot, and for one delirious moment I thought the airbed was coming too. But instead the beach ball emerged, along with my bright orange armbands. He threw the latter to me to blow up as he strode through the sand dunes, me running along beside. There was hardly anyone else to be seen as we crossed the golden sand down to the sea, our tracks cutting across the beach in a diagonal line.

Dropping my bag not far from the edge of the shore, I raced into the water, shouting and laughing, kicking and splashing. My father soon followed me in, his hairy white body exposed in his swimming trunks.

We played more games together that evening in the cold Atlantic than I'd ever played with him before: water fights, jumping the waves, water polo with the beach ball. Usually I was left in the shallows when he went off for a swim, but tonight he took me with him out to the biggest waves, holding me in front as they broke over us. Before leaving we sat together in the shallows, feeling the waves lapping gently against us.

It was time to go. We picked up our clothes, and he carried me on his shoulders back up the beach and into the sand dunes, his feet alone making tracks in the sand where before there had been two.

He found a quiet spot in the dunes where we could get changed. I was getting cold now and looking forward to having some proper clothes on again. I slipped my arms out of the swimming costume and pulled it down towards my belly. I rubbed at my skin with the scratchy stripy towel my mother had given me. I pulled my white vest over my head before trying to fasten the towel round my waist. Usually my mother did this bit for me—I had not yet mastered the art of rolling the towel down and in to get it to hold tight.

I was suddenly aware of my father watching me. He'd already swapped his swimming trunks for light cotton trousers. *Oh God, he's going to be angry with me for keeping him waiting*, I thought. I fumbled faster with the towel.

"Here, let me help you with that," he said.

I was taken aback by his friendly offer of assistance. Soon he had the towel secure around my waist. I started carefully to pull down my swimming costume, not wanting to expose myself, even though there was no one around but my father.

"I might as well finish the job," he said, stepping forward.

I was not used to anyone helping me to get changed. According to my mother, I'd started trying to dress myself from the minute I could stand. By the time I was two she had no part in it at all; I'd come downstairs in the morning fully dressed, waiting only for her to tie my shoelaces. My father had never dressed me.

But here he was pulling down my bathing costume. I wanted to say, "I can do it myself," as I did when my mother tried to intervene in my struggles. "I'm not a baby." But I knew better than to say anything to my father. A quick slap on the bare legs would have been the result. Anyway, the stupid costume would be off in a minute and I'd be able to finish dressing myself.

But the stupid costume wasn't off in a minute. It was pulled down only a short way and then I felt my father's hand push its way between my legs. I flinched away but he pulled me roughly back towards him and knelt down, pinning me to his chest.

A sharp pain brought tears to my eyes as his fingers forced their way inside my body. His face was almost next to mine, and I heard his breath quicken in my ear. I glanced at him, wishing this wasn't happening, hoping it wasn't him. His cold green eyes bored into me, his tongue licking away the sweat that had broken out on his top lip.

I closed my eyes and turned my head away, unable to face his face. Tears pricked out from between my shut lids.

I don't know how long we stayed there like that. It seemed like for ever, but it can only have been a few minutes. A few minutes that changed my childhood, changed my life.

Still kneeling, he finally removed my wet bathing costume and thrust it into my arms. "Not a word to anyone. I'm warning you." Then he turned his back on me and finished getting dressed.

I, too, must have finished dressing, though I don't remember it. I don't remember putting my clothes on, wrapping my costume in my towel, putting them in the bag. I don't remember walking to the car, getting in and driving home. I don't remember anything else of that evening.

All I remember is standing in the sand dunes, the scratchy stripy towel still hung around my waist, clutching my ruffled blue bathing costume to my chest, tears rolling down my cheeks, pain searing between my legs.

But then I've always been a little forgetful, always had a lot to forget.

Chapter 1

Hoots, man

HE WAS A funny man, my dad. As in peculiar.

A man of changing passions, gusting over him, and us, in passing phases. When I was eight, he decided that he was Scottish. The fact that he was Belfast born and bred, Irish for generations back, was a minor detail. Never let the truth get in the way of a good story. And being Scottish was the latest story my dad wanted to tell.

We were on a family holiday at the time. He started speaking with a Scottish accent, singing Scottish songs, playing Scottish music and reading Robbie Burns. "Och aye the noo" and "hoots man" peppered his conversation.

The holiday wasn't even in Scotland but on a caravan park in north-east England. It was packed to the gunnels with Scottish families. A day trip to Edinburgh tipped him over the edge. He found a coat of arms for the MacCullochs in a tartan shop just off the Royal Mile and decided that our Irish name, McCullagh, could just as easily be this Scottish one. On our return to Ireland, he gave it pride of place in the hallway.

He also brought back a leaflet from a kilt manufacturer. Over the next few years, he was to become one of their best-ever customers, tissue-wrapped tartan arriving by mail order at our home in Coleraine, County Londonderry.

The first one came on a Saturday morning in November 1973. I was playing ludo with my best friend Clare in the sitting room when my dad came in. "What do yese think, lassies?" he said in his Scots accent.

Clare had asked me about the accent before, but I'd pretended I didn't know what she was talking about. But this time there could be no pretending. He stood before us in black brogues, cream knee socks and a red, green and blue tartan kilt. A black beret with a bluish feather perched jauntily on the side of his head, and a brown leather sporran swung before him as he twirled a couple of times to give us the full effect.

"Eh, Constance? Clare? What do yese think?"

I couldn't think. All I could do was stare.

Luckily Clare replied, "It's very nice, Mr McCullagh. Nice, erm, check."

"Aye, it's the MacCulloch tartan," he said. "Our family tartan. We're one of the auldest and most noble o' all the Scottish clans. So ye like it, Clare? What about you Constance? I've no heard your verdict."

I wanted to shout, "Have you completely lost your marbles?" Instead I said, "It's really… really great."

He nodded briefly. "Aye, that it is. But hoots, man, I've no time to be spending the morning chatting. I've things tae do." And with that he was off.

One kilt proved not to satisfy his taste for tartan. The following month another special delivery arrived. This time it was the Bonnie Prince Charlie package: an eight-yard kilt in MacCulloch dress tartan, black velvet dress jacket, white pleated shirt, sealskin sporran, dancing pumps and a jewelled dagger to wear down his sock.

He enlisted the whole family in his new identity. He

bought my mum a knee-length kilt for daytime and a full-length one for the weekly Scottish dancing classes he enrolled them in. She drew the line, however, at inserting "och aye" into every fourth sentence.

I, too, received a kilt and was expected to support Scotland over Ireland at football and rugby. My sister, Joanna, was already tartanned up. She was in her Bay City Rollers phase and had a pair of white Les McKeown baggy trousers with tartan stripes down the side and a tartan-lined bomber jacket. My dad completed her look with a thin MacCulloch tartan scarf to tie round her wrist. Simon, my brother, was enrolled as a junior member of the Scottish Nationalist Party.

On evenings out, dressed in his kilt and sporran, his velvet jacket and his frilly shirt, his dagger and his dancing shoes, my father would slip into his Scots accent: "Och, hen, cannie I get ye a wee dram?" Some people were taken in. On New Year's Eve, as my dad sang "Flower of Scotland" at the Coleraine Rugby Club dinner dance, a man asked my mother, "Why did your husband ever leave Scotland, when he obviously loves it so much?" But in a town as small as Coleraine, I think most knew the truth, and I'd change the subject if anyone ever mentioned Scotland.

My father's Scottish identity determined the destination of our annual summer holiday for several years—not by holidaying actually in Scotland, but by returning to the place where he'd discovered his Scottish identity. Haggerston Castle caravan park put my dad close to his obsession, but it ruined my own passion of the time: the Wombles.

I loved the Wombles. Huge, great, grey, furry creatures, they were the highlight of my day. On weekdays before the BBC News, I made sure to finish my chores so that I could watch them without being called upon to lay the table or wash the potatoes. Underground, overground, I was their greatest fan. Uncle Bulgaria, Madame Cholet, Tomsk, Tobermory, Orinoco—I loved them all. They were the family I really wanted. But over the course of our second Haggerston holiday in 1974, I lost them.

Our preparations for Haggerston began weeks in advance with my mother sifting through our clothes and setting aside those we would be taking. Food began to be stockpiled, as if England still operated under a rationing system and we needed enough supplies to last the fortnight.

The day before our departure, my dad wheeled the trailer round to the front of the house for loading. By accident he put it down on his foot, and as a result he could not participate in the loading. Instead he shouted instructions to my harassed mother and the rest of us, over "I Belong to Glasgow", which was blaring out from the record player.

"Och, Maisie. Jeesus Christ. I didnae tell ye tae take that yin. I tellt ye tae take that other yin there.

"Simon, do ye no ken how tae load properly? Ye're wandering aroon like some great fairy.

"If it wasnae for this bad foot, I'd hae finished this in half the time it's taken yese."

Eventually the loading was complete, and he limped outside to secure the tarpaulin in place.

We set off the following evening. My father wanted to wear a kilt for the journey, but my mother persuaded him that it might get dirty on the boat. He made do with red tartan trousers, black polo shirt, red V-neck and green tartan tam-o'-shanter.

The ferry was packed, but eventually we found somewhere

to sit and settled down to share a flask of soup and some corned beef sandwiches my mother had made. It was a bad start: I hated corned beef and the soup was lukewarm.

I was soon bored, sitting with my family, listening to my dad singing Scottish songs under his breath and my mum tutting at a group of Belfast kids running up and down the gangway, shouting and screaming. It was a relief when Scotland was sighted up ahead. My father took us out on deck.

"Aye, it's oor homeland. Isnae it beautiful?" he said.

It was some time before we finally docked and even longer waiting in the hold of the ship to disembark. As we drove off the ferry, my father insisted we all join in on a rousing chorus of "Scotland the Brave".

We drove into the night, and I fell asleep sitting upright between my brother and sister. I woke briefly when we parked up in a lay-by for Dad to get some sleep, then slept through till dawn. We peed behind a hedge, then ate more of the corned beef sandwiches before setting off on the last part of the journey.

By a quarter past nine, we were unloading the trailer into our Haggerston caravan, and soon we were settled down to sausages, bacon, fried biscuits (one of my mother's specialities—on this occasion Rich Tea) and toast.

It was a great first day. I messed around with Joanna in the playground, came out ahead on the camp slot machines and cheered my dad on to victory in the talent contest at the camp dance that evening. He had the voice of Joseph Locke, and "Scotland the Brave" went down a storm.

He was in a good mood the next morning.

"Ah, it was some night, eh?" he said, as we sat down to our Shreddies.

I nodded.

"Where's my toast, Maisie?" he called. "This is my celebration breakfast."

He turned back to Simon, Joanna and me and sang:

> "Land of my heart for ever
> Scotland the braaaaaaaaave.

"Aye, some night indeed. But next Saturday's going to be even better. Do yese want to know why?"

No one answered.

"I said do yese want to know why?"

"Why?" my sister said.

"Well, next weekend, not only will I be winning, but one of you will be too."

"One of us?" I said.

"Aye, you're all entering the junior competition. Sure, if you've even half my talent, you're guaranteed victory. Just think what Pat and Seamus will have to say to that."

Pat and Seamus were our next-door neighbours, the O'Briens. They were joining us for the second week of our holiday in the next-door caravan.

As the week progressed, I still didn't know what I was going to do. My mother suggested that I recite a poem, but I did not think that would be much of a crowd-pleaser. Joanna had decided on an Irish jig, but Simon was refusing to enter at all.

"Ach, ye've no talent anyway, ye great jessie," my father said. "I dinnae need you. My wee lassies will win it for me. They will nae let me doon."

All entrants had to register by midday on the morning of the competition. There were two categories—eleven and

over, and ten and under. Joanna and I joined the queue trick-
ling out of the dance hall. I was going with my mother's sug-
gestion of a poem, one I'd learned about mice. The first line
was, "I think mice are rather nice."

I knew it wasn't a winner, but at least my dad would know
I'd tried. When my sister went forward and gave her name—
Joanna McCullagh; age: 12; performance: Irish tap danc-
ing—I was still with the mice.

> Their tails are long their faces small
> They haven't any chins at all.

Joanna got her slip of paper and left me to register on my
own. The bleached blonde taking the names beckoned me
forward. And instead of giving my details as Constance
McCullagh; age: 8; performance: reciting "Mice are Nice", I'd
transformed into Constance McCullagh; age: 8; singing
"Remember You're a Womble".

I don't know what made me do it, where the idea even
came from. I'd thought of singing but had not been able to
think of the right song—"Twinkle Twinkle Little Star" was not
going to propel me to stardom. So I left the hall thrilled by
my last-minute stroke of genius.

I decided not to tell my family of the change of plan, so I
kept my slip of paper to myself. It would reinforce my
moment of triumph if no one knew it was coming. My only
disappointment was that I did not have a grey furry outfit.
Still, I knew people would love the song so much that the lack
of a costume wouldn't count against me.

All day I secretly practised. In my head during lunch, out
loud when I went on my own for a walk, back in my head
when the O'Briens arrived just after three o'clock, and out

loud again when I went to buy sweets from the camp shop. When I got to the chorus, "Remember you're a womble", I could hear the audience joining in with gusto.

I started to get nervous as I changed into my best dress, a long pink gingham.

Don't worry, I told myself. *Everyone loves the Wombles. You're going to win.*

It was a warm summer's evening, and I carried my cardigan as we walked up to the hall with the O'Briens. There were six O'Briens—Mr and Mrs, Patrick, 14, Gerald, 13, Mary, 11, and Joseph, 10. We were early for once and found two tables together near to the front with a good view of the stage. Mr O'Brien bought me a Fanta, and I sipped it through a straw while I waited for the competition to start.

I was fifth on. I'd always liked the number five and took this as a good sign. Soon it was my big moment. I walked forward and handed my slip of paper to the MC, a large, slightly sweating man in a gold lurex dinner jacket.

"And now we have Constance McCullagh, aged 8, with"— and here there was a slight pause and a definite smirk— "'Remember You're a Womble'. Take it away, Constance."

I was singing unaccompanied—the band did not have the music for "Remember You're a Womble". I took the microphone in my hand and began to sing. The audience was silent as I began the first verse, but I knew I'd have them with me come the chorus.

"Remember you're a womble," I sang out, clear and sure, ready for their answering "Remember you're a womble". Only it didn't come.

I began to lose confidence as I began the second line of the chorus, an octave higher than the first.

"Remember you're a womble," I squeaked, half waving my arm in a vain attempt to get the audience to join in. By the time I got to "Remember, member, member, what a womble, womble, womble you are", my voice was beginning to break.

I looked towards my family for support. Quite why, I don't know. Other than my mother, they'd always been a bunch of bastards. My mum was engaged in a whispered conversation with Joanna, and the rest of the table were openly laughing. I was on my own.

There were two more verses to "Remember You're a Womble". They were bad enough. But the choruses in between were pure purgatory. By the final one, even the MC was urging the audience to join in. A few people did, but not enough to make a difference.

I returned to my family table where they were still laughing at my performance. My mother asked, "What made you choose that song?" But I had no answer so I stayed quiet.

I was quiet for most of the evening, spending long periods hiding in the toilets. But there was no escape on the way home. I didn't like the walk from the dance hall to our caravan at the best of times. I was terrified of the dark, and the barely lit path took you past an old, abandoned building. I was sure that there were dead bodies buried there. I'd dreamt about them a few nights before, rising up out of their graves and swooping down to attack me in my bed. Normally I'd stick close to my family, but tonight I walked ahead, tuning out their chatter. As I approached the building, I began to slow. What if the ghosts were in there? What if they got me?

I heard my dad call my name. I looked round. "Remember you're a womble," he sang in a screechy, tuneless voice.

I wanted to run, away from him, away from everything. But I was scared of the deep shadows, the ghosts ahead, and of how much trouble I'd be in if I ran.

My feet didn't move. Instead I turned my head away. My family had caught up with me by now. I started to walk. Every few steps, one or other of my father, my brother, my sister or the O'Brien children would call, "Constance," and then sing-song "Remember you're a womble" at the top of their voices.

It was a relief to get back to the caravan and the relative sanctuary of the bunk room that I shared with my sister. I slipped into the lower bunk, shutting the night and my family out.

Chapter 2

Aunt Gertrude

I HOPED I'D be able to leave my wombling humiliation behind when we returned to Ireland, but my dad had other ideas, as I discovered when my Aunt Gertrude came to visit.

Gertrude was my father's much older sister. Odd as my father could be, he was only a beginner compared to Aunt Gertrude. She had the look of a weirdo, someone you wouldn't choose to sit next to on the bus. Her hair was pulled back in a severe and unflattering bun. Pale-green, watery eyes peered out at you from behind thick, blue-rimmed NHS spectacles. She blinked often, flaring her nostrils and pushing out her top lip at the same time. Although a deeply religious woman, she seemed not to have heard of "cleanliness is next to godliness"; a strange air of mothballs and mildew hung about her person and unidentified fragments clung to her teeth.

Even though she was family, I always found her a bit creepy. Her husband Jim wasn't much better; greasy hair, bad breath and buck teeth did not add up to a friendly uncle face.

They belonged to the ultra-strict Cooneyite sect, one of Northern Ireland's many sub-species of Protestant. Jehovah's Witnesses, Mormons, Plymouth Brethren, Free

Presbyterians—we had them all and more. My family were common or garden Presbyterians with a commitment to duty, hard work and an avoidance of pleasure if you wanted to escape eternal damnation and the fires of hell.

I didn't know the ins and outs of the Cooneyite take on God but wondered if it might be behind Aunt Gertrude's strangeness.

"Well, I'm sure it hasn't helped, but Constance, to be honest, Gertrude's always been strange," my mum explained. "When we were young, a load of us used to go up to the dances on a Saturday evening. But not Gertrude. No. Every Saturday evening, she used to take her knitting in a string bag and go and sit on a bench at the Clock, watching the prostitutes."

I'd heard of prostitutes on *Kojak*. I didn't know exactly what they did, but I knew it wasn't good. I imagined my aunt sitting under a streetlight, needles clicking back and forth, contentedly watching some bad business.

We saw Aunt Gertrude only occasionally. They lived in Lisburn, sixty miles away, and visits were restricted by my aunt and uncle's limited availability. Uncle Jim usually worked on a Saturday, and Sundays were given over to the Lord. But as luck would have it, they were on an evangelical soul-saving mission in Castlerock the week after we came back from Haggerston and my mum invited them for tea on the Sunday.

Sunday mornings were always frantic in our house. Church attendance, though not necessarily religious belief, was a requirement when I was growing up. My mum attached a great deal of significance to the appearance of our hair for church. But despite weekly experience of how long it took to do, she'd never leave enough time. This morning was no different.

We were already running late when my mum started taking out my sister's curlers. Joanna fidgeted as my mum coaxed and cajoled her hair away from its usual taily appearance.

"Will you stand still, for God's sake. I'm having to work miracles here as it is without you jigging about like a hen on a griddle. Honestly, Joanna, it's like rats' tails. You'll end up with a ball of hair in your stomach if you don't stop sucking it. You'll only have yourself to blame if they have to cut you open to get it out."

Her hands darted about my sister's hair for a few more minutes.

"Right. Well, that will have to do. Constance, your turn. Come on, hurry up or you'll be late."

She began to claw a vicious steel comb through my long hair. I winced as my mum went in for the kill. With a final flourish of the comb, she pulled my face an inch higher and stapled a clip into the top of my head to hold the hair in place.

"Go and find your father. You'll need a lift if it's to be worth going at all."

I hated getting a lift from my dad. He was always dressed in his oldest, dirtiest clothes first thing on a Sunday morning, and I worried about who might see him.

"Do we have to go? Why can't we go to Aunt Gertrude's service instead?" I asked.

"What do you want to go and sit in a tent on the beach for when you could be snug in First Coleraine?"

"But it would be exciting," I said. "They might even have competitions."

I loved religious competitions, ever since I'd joined the Good News Club the year before. The club had been set up by our Plymouth Brethren neighbour Mrs Craig and her friend Mrs Watson, in the latter's front room. I'd not really joined for the religion. No, I'd been intrigued by the prospect of seeing Mrs Craig out in the afternoon. She usually sat at home in the dark with the curtains closed. My mother thought it was her nerves, but I knew she was secretly watching the horse racing on the television.

My joining the club turned out not to be good news for Mrs Craig's daughter, Laura. Up until that point, she'd usually won the weekly Bible quiz at the Club. But I discovered that my capacity for memorising religious trivia was immense. The age of Methuselah (969), the shortest verse in the Bible (Jesus wept), the chosen ones who survived Nebuchadnezzar's fiery furnace (Shadrach, Meshach and Abednego)—my finger was on the buzzer for these and many more. I think that the emergence of a mere Presbyterian as Bible knowledge champion was something of a disappointment to Mrs Craig, who stopped helping out at the group after only a few weeks.

"I don't think Gertrude's the competition type. Now go and get your father."

By the time we arrived at Sunday school, the hum of catechism had already descended across the hall. I joined my group and got down to work.

After Sunday school, Joanna and I made our way to our usual pew at the front of the upstairs gallery of the church, facing the pulpit. At twenty-five past eleven, the choir, in their burgundy robes, filed into the seats in front of the organ. My dad was amongst them. A minute later my mum joined us, stepping cautiously down the stairs to our pew in black court shoes and a wide-brimmed red hat flecked with black dots.

My mum didn't always come to church, depending on how much of a grip she had on Sunday dinner. To be honest, I preferred it without her—she sang as if her life depended on drowning out the rest of the church. I glanced at the hymn board and my heart sank as I spotted number 51. "O God our help in ages past" was always full force.

At 11.30 our minister, the Reverend Colin Lightfoot, emerged through the door to the left of the pulpit and climbed the stairs to take his place in front of the congregation. I was a bit nervous of the Rev. Lightfoot. The previous January, I'd been trudging home from school through driving rain when he stopped his car beside me.

"It's Constance, isn't it? Get in and I'll give you a lift home."

But my mum had warned me on pain of death not to get into a car with any man (except, of course, my dad) without checking with her.

"No, thank you," I said. "I'm not allowed."

"But you're getting soaked. Your mum won't mind."

"No thanks, sir. Really, I'm not allowed."

In the end he gave up and drove off, and I carried on walking, needles of rain stinging my face. I felt a twinge of anxiety when I spotted his car in front of our house as I tramped up the last stretch home. But how could I be in trouble? I'd done what my mum had told me to.

I heard laughter from the lounge, our posh room, as I came through the kitchen. I crept towards the hatch, a small wooden door halfway up the wall between the kitchen and the lounge. More laughter, but I couldn't make out the words.

I went into the hall and hung up my dripping anorak.

"Is that you, Constance?" my mum called.

"Yes."

"Come on in." I felt my face redden as I pushed open the door. "You can talk to the minister while I go and make some tea."

"I see you've made it home safely," the Rev. Lightfoot said. I nodded.

"I hope I didn't upset you back there," he said. "The Bible says to honour your father and mother. You did very well to follow what your parents had said."

Obedience was the theme of today's service, too, with Jonah's stopover in the belly of a whale as a cautionary tale. We went home after the service to Scotch broth and bread, instead of our usual roast. Then my mum set about preparing an afternoon tea spread for Gertrude, Jim and their teenage daughter Miriam.

They arrived later that afternoon in a battered blue Reliant Robin. My aunt shuffled up the driveway, five string bags clutched about her person. It was close to my birthday, and she fished a present out of one of them and handed it to me.

"Happy Birthday, Constance," she whined.

I didn't hold out much hope for the present as I began to unwrap it. I think she used to buy them at the market in Lisburn (where she also maintained her supply of string bags), and the strangest things seemed to catch her eye. The previous year she'd sent me a large green glass stone encased in a gold nylon mesh suspended from a gold bouclé nylon chain. The stone was so heavy that it left a bruise when I made the mistake of running with it on.

Today it was a toothbrush and a spool of navy blue thread.

"Thanks, Auntie," I said.

We'd barely sat down to tea when my dad launched into his wombling story.

"Ah, you should have seen the fool our Constance made of herself on holiday. You should have been there, Gertrude. You know that song 'Remember You're a Womble'?" He paused. My aunt looked at him blankly.

"Ah, you must know it." I stared down at my ham sandwich as he sang the first line of the chorus—"Remember you're a womble."

He turned to Miriam.

"You must know the Wombles, Miriam. You know, off the television."

"Victor, you know we don't hold with that instrument of sin," my aunt said, cutting my father off at the knees. "Now we've something far more important to talk about than all this nonsense. Congratulations are in order. Miriam's betrothed."

I looked at my blushing cousin in amazement. She was wearing a bottle-green, ankle-length tent of a dress, her long dark hair pinned up in its usual bun. She'd inherited my uncle's protruding buck teeth and my aunt's weak eyes. Her expression was gormless. Still only fifteen, her face was ravaged by teenage acne. From the outside she certainly didn't look capable of attracting a man.

I think the rest of my family must have been having similar thoughts because there was a momentary pause before my mother spluttered, "Congratulations, Miriam. He's a very lucky man."

Miriam giggled.

"So what's he like? What's his name?" my mum politely continued.

Miriam giggled again.

"He's a fine, upstanding young man. Luke Hill. He's been in our church a long time. Even taught Miriam here in Bible study class," Uncle Jim said.

"Luke. I've always liked that name," my mum said to Miriam. "So how did he propose?"

"He came to me," my uncle answered. "And I had no doubt. Not in a man of his quality."

My mother made one last effort with Miriam.

"So what does he do?"

Miriam glanced towards my uncle and he nodded his permission.

"He's a milkman," she answered. "He delivers milk."

And this was as much as my mother got out of her about her future husband over tea. My sister found out a little more in our bedroom later that afternoon: he'd a nice smile, he lived with his widowed mother, he was thirty years old, they would marry in the summer when my cousin had come of age.

The invite arrived in March of the following year. My father opened it, reading it over breakfast. He threw the invite on to the table.

"That bloody witch. Who the hell does she think she is?"

"What is it, Victor?"

"Gertrude. That bloody freak of a sister of mine. Look at that invite."

My mother picked it up and began to read, eyes flicking back and forth across the words. She looked nervously towards my father.

"Jesus, woman. Look at the order of service—it's on the back."

My mother turned the invite over and began scanning.

"I didn't know you were singing," she said.

"No, neither did I. How dare she? She thinks I'm still her little brother to be bossed around. Well, she can think again. I'm not bloody well doing it."

"Now, Victor. Don't be hasty."

But my father's mind was made up. Not only was he not singing, but he wasn't going either. None of us were. He screwed the invitation up and flung it into the bin.

It meant I didn't know the date for the wedding. Not until 7 July. We were sitting down to tea—sausages, chips and beans—when the phone rang.

"Ah Jesus, who the hell's that?" my father said. But he got up anyway. He left the door open as he went to answer the mustard phone in the hallway. I heard his standard: "Coleraine 3874, McCullagh speaking."

His side of the conversation, at least, was strange.

"So you're using Satan's instrument.

"No, we're all fine.

"Because it's time you stopped thinking you own me."

Then he put the phone down.

He came back in. "That was Gertrude," he said and laughed.

"Gertrude?" my mum said. "I thought she didn't believe in the phone."

"She doesn't usually, but she seemed to think this was some kind of emergency."

"Has something happened?"

"Something and nothing. Miriam was married today. Gertrude phoned to check we were all right. She couldn't see what else would keep us away. I soon put her straight." He laughed again, and I felt a tiny shiver. "I think she's learned her lesson this time."

Still smiling, he sat down and started to cut up his sausages.

Chapter 3

Bloody Friday

THE YEAR 1972 was a bloody one in Northern Ireland. From Bloody Sunday through Bloody Friday and countless bombings and shootings in between, more than 450 people died. Night after night of explosion after explosion on the TV. And it wasn't just the news—I'd be watching *The Generation Game* when Bruce would be cut off.

"We would like to interrupt this broadcast to request that all keyholders in Magherafelt [or Newry or Strabane or wherever else they'd chosen that night] return to their premises."

From the Abercorn to Newry to Claudy, blood was spilling out everywhere. But Bloody Friday was the worst of all: thirty bombs in forty minutes, nine people dead. We were in Belfast that day. My parents were both Belfast born and bred, and most of our relatives still lived there. We'd go and visit about once a month, usually on a Sunday. But on Friday, 21 July 1972, the day that turned out to be Bloody Friday, we'd gone up to do some shopping.

We were due to set off after breakfast that Friday, but half an hour later we were still at home. My mother was fussing over my hair and insisting on a dress.

"Your granda doesn't want to see you running around like a tomboy," she said.

Joanna had already endured the same performance, and even Simon had to comb his hair and put on his "tidy trousers"—a pair of dark brown flares—a beige shirt with long pointy collar and a chocolate, beige and orange-striped tank top.

At last we set off. But we got only as far as the post box on the corner of the next road before my mother said, "Oh, no. Victor, I don't know if I switched off the iron." We nearly always returned home at least once before really getting under way, for scones or coconut haystacks or whatever else my mother had baked for my grandparents, or to check whether the bath was still running or the frying pan still on.

"Ah Jesus, Maisie. Have you any bloody brain at all?" my father guldered as he spun the car on two wheels into a U-turn and accelerated back to the house. My mum sat silent as his torrent of abuse swept round the car.

We screeched to a halt halfway up the drive. My mum got out, adopting that half-run used by so many women of any age after adolescence, especially when wearing a dress, like the muscles have forgotten what it's like to let loose and run free. Then she was fumbling for her key and struggling with the door before disappearing from view.

She'd been in the house only about thirty seconds when he started to beep the horn. It was intermittent at first, punctuated with, "In the name of God, what's keeping her? Maisie, come on. What are you at? Come on, come on, come on."

Then he gave one long continuous blast on the horn. I saw the next-door neighbours' curtains twitching and looked at my lap. Still she did not return. He leapt out of the car and sprinted up to the house. He was fumbling for his key in his pocket with one hand, ringing the doorbell repeatedly with the other. I could hear him shouting, "Ah Jesus, will you hurry up, Maisie. What the fuck are you doing in there?"

Suddenly my mother reappeared, hot and flustered, and made her way back to the car, ignoring my father as best she could.

Belfast was just over fifty miles away. We were about eight miles into the journey when a red car overtook us on the stretch between Ballymoney and Ballymena. My dad started to accelerate. "Catch 'em. Catch 'em. I'm gonna catch 'em," he chanted as we closed in on the bumper of the offending vehicle. Then he swerved out into the opposing lane, accelerated past the red car and shot back into our own lane just in front of it.

"Hurray," we cheered, as expected. We'd been through "catch 'em" before. Depending on his mood, he might slow down now, speeding up only if the car behind tried to overtake. Or he might drive normally. During the day, you never could be sure. It was a different story at night. Once dusk had fallen, he was a very careful driver. A couple of years earlier, an Ulsterbus had burst into flames just ahead of us as we came round a corner on the back road near Cullybackey one night. My dad almost lost control of the car, swerving across the road, branches of the hedge rapping against the roof and windows. We were lucky there was nothing coming in the opposite direction. He'd been careful at night ever since.

Today he drove normally, the rest of the journey to Belfast was uneventful and Joanna and I passed the time playing cat's cradle and I spy. We pulled up outside my grandparents' house just before eleven. It was a two-up, two-down red-brick Corporation house on Mountcollyer Road in north Belfast.

They'd been there since they married in 1925. We were bare-ly in the door before my granny was off making a cup of tea. My mum protested. "Ah, Mummy, we've not really time for tea. We should be off up the town."

"Not have tea?" my granny said. "Sure you need something to sustain you. It'll only take me a couple of min-utes. I've already the kettle boiled. I'll just put the pot on to draw."

My granny considered the drinking of tea as a necessity for sustaining life, almost on a par with eating and breathing. But I'd yet to like it. Last time we visited, my granda had tried to pass off a glass of cold tea as coke. He did it as a joke, but as he saw me force each sip down, he came over and took the glass from me. "I'll bring you some orange juice instead," he said.

I had orange juice again today while everyone else start-ed on cups of strong tea.

"I've brought a wee bit of Battenberg to go along with it," my granny said, handing out plates of chequered pink and yellow cake. My granny hated to have anyone cross her threshold without feeding them. On Sundays she'd always have the dinner on when we arrived around midday. And it would always be the same thing: a field of boiled potatoes, mince and gravy, and tinned carrots and peas. We'd eat as soon as my granda arrived back from church. The meat and potatoes were always followed by tinned fruit with evaporat-ed milk, though the variety of fruit changed from visit to visit—peaches or pears or fruit salad with a battle for the glacé cherry.

After tea and Battenberg, my parents, Joanna and Simon set off for the bus into town. I stayed with my grandparents.

I loved spending time with them, especially my granda. As soon as my parents had gone, I slipped over to his rocking chair and he lifted me on to his lap. I loved it up on my granda's lap, playing with his glasses, the buttons on his cardigan, his gold watch. Even after I gave him a black eye, accidentally clattering him in the face with my elbow as I fidgeted about, he was still happy to have me clamber up to chatter and laugh and joke with him. I learned to read young, before I went to school, and he'd beam down upon me as I read him the sports page from his newspaper.

"Your granny's just going to make the dinner," he said. "What shall we do?"

"Oh," I said, "is there anything in the cupboard?"

The cupboard lay behind a latched wooden door next to my granda's rocking chair in the corner of the sitting room. It was built deep into the wall, and all sorts could emerge from it: playing cards, photos, buttons and string, paper and pens, old keys and coins. He took out some of the coins, paper and a couple of pencils.

"See this one," he said. He handed me an old brown coin about an inch across. "Do you see the date on it?"

I searched the surface. "1903," I said.

"That was the year I was born. That's an old penny."

"Have you one for 1965, the year I was born?" He chuckled, then searched through his collection. "Here you go. Now put the coin under the paper." I did as he said. "Take your pencil and colour gently over the coin."

"Oh, I like that," I said as a copy of the coin appeared on my sheet. I spent twenty minutes happily making coin patterns till my granny called us for dinner: chips and fried peas with slices of buttered white bread. We ate as usual in the pantry, a small room off the tiny scullery where my granny prepared the food.

After lunch I helped clear the plates for my granda to do the dishes. The scullery had the only running water in the house, a cold tap with a rubber nozzle on the end, and a long thin pipe, hovering above the sink, which linked to an ancient geyser that heated the water.

"Thanks, love," he said. "You go out and play in the yard for five minutes. Once I've done the dishes, we'll go to the park. I'll bring some of that leftover bread for the ducks."

There wasn't a lot of space in the yard, but I practised a few Irish dancing steps that Mary O'Brien had been teaching Joanna and me. The yard was flanked by eight-foot high walls, topped with glass shards. The back wall had a door to the entry, a narrow passage running down the back of the houses. I could hear the sounds of children playing in the playground on North Queen Street on the other side of the entry. And the buzz of an army helicopter overhead.

"All right, I'm done now. Why don't you go to the toilet, and then we'll be off," my granda said. I didn't like my grandparents' toilet. It was in the yard next to the coal hole, and I worried about creepy-crawlies.

We set off about half past one, down Mountcollyer Road, me hopping and skipping along beside my granda.

"Oh, you're full of life today," he said. "An old man like me can hardly keep up."

We turned left at the corner on to North Queen Street and followed the road for ten minutes to the Grove Park.

"Do you want to go to the playground first or shall we feed the ducks?"

"Oh, the ducks, please."

My granda had taught me to identify mallard ducks, but he didn't know the name of some white ducks that were new to the pond. Five little mottled-brown ducklings followed one of the mallards. I threw some bread towards them. We were just sprinkling the last crumbs on to the bank when a huge bang thumped out from the city centre.

"That was a bomb, wasn't it, Granda? Where do you think it was?"

"I don't know. It sounded towards the centre."

We carried on through the park, towards the playground. But then another massive blast swallowed up the park.

"There's another one," he said. "I think we'd best get back home."

I trotted along beside him as we made our way out of the park. We'd not even reached the gates when a third explosion burst out from the city centre. We quickened our pace along North Queen Street. As we passed the end of Deacon Street, where my other granny lived, a fourth bomb went off. On we went, past the playground to the bottom of Mountcollyer Road, as a fire engine rocketed past us, sirens wailing.

Usually on our journey back from the park we carried straight on past Mountcollyer Road to the bakery on the Limestone Road where my Aunt Edie worked. She'd give me a jam tart to eat on the way home and put some bread and cakes in a bag for my granda. But not today. Today we went straight home.

As we turned into Mountcollyer Road, another blast crashed out. My granda broke into a run. My granny was standing at the gate looking down the street.

"Is Maisie back?" my granda asked.

"No," my granny replied. "Not yet."

"Let's go in."

Another explosion, the loudest yet, and my granny was back out at the gate, with me just behind.

"Where are they? Where are they?" I could hear her repeating as she peered down the street. Plumes of black smoke were visible in the distance.

"Are they going to be OK, Granny? Are they going to be all right?" I was beginning to panic now, feeling the fear from my grandmother. I screamed as another bomb went off, the closest yet.

"Where's Mummy? When's she going to be home?"

My granda came out to us.

"Come on in now. You can't do anything standing at the gate. Come on in, Peggy. Can't you see you're frightening the child."

My granny turned reluctantly from the gate and went back into the house. Both the television and radio were on. "Away and make us all a cup of tea," my granda said to her. She went obediently into the kitchen and put the kettle on to boil.

Another explosion.

My granda fiddled with the radio channels. "Reports are coming in of a series of explosions in Belfast. Emergency services are on the scene. Eyewitness reports suggest heavy casualties, but we have no official confirmation. No one has yet claimed responsibility."

"The Fenian bastards," muttered my granda. "May they rot in hell."

Before he could say any more, we heard the front gate open. He rushed to the door, expecting my parents, brother and sister, but it was only Frankie Nelson from three doors down.

"Have you heard anything?" my granda asked.

Frankie was one of the few people in the area to own a phone and was often used to pass messages to other people in the street.

"I'm afraid not, Michael. I know your Maisie's up for the day. I saw her heading into town earlier."

Another explosion and my granny was back into the front room.

"I just can't believe this," Frankie said. "They've got to do something."

As the kettle came to the boil, my granny went back to the scullery. She put the teapot on the stove to draw and returned to the front room with a tray of rock cakes and a glass of orange juice.

She was just getting the cups down for the tea when another bomb went off and she dropped one. It smashed on to the scullery floor. My granny started to cry as she fumbled around trying to pick up the pieces of the broken cup.

"Oh, dear God. Please get them home safe. Please, God."

Frankie went to help her.

"Don't worry, Peggy," he said. "I'm sure Maisie's fine. She'll be home soon."

"I hope you're right, Frankie. I hope to God you're right."

I was crying too by now. "I want Mummy home, Granda. When are they going to come?"

"I don't know," he said, coming over and sitting beside me on the sofa. "Come on now, calm yourself. Your mummy wouldn't want you getting yourself upset. Calm down and have something to eat, there's a good girl."

I started to eat one of the rock cakes my mum had brought with her that morning, slowly chewing. I'd eaten only half of it when another bomb went off.

It felt like it would never end. But it did. The last bomb went off just before three, though it was some time before we realised it had been the last. The sirens continued to wail, the helicopters whirred overhead, but the devastating blasts were over.

There was still no sign of my mother. My granda scanned the radio for news. My granny fidgeted with her apron, occasionally going to look out the window. Frankie went home to wait by the phone.

Just after half past four, the gate clicked again, and suddenly my mother, father, brother and sister were pouring through the front door, filling up the room. My granny had my mum in her arms—"Thank God, thank God, thank God", she kept repeating. It was some minutes before she let her go, but eventually my mum was able to sit down. She took me on to her lap.

"Oh, thank God to be home," she said. "I've never seen anything like it, and pray God I never do again."

"Your mummy was worried sick about you," my granda said. "All them bombs and then hearing about casualties on the radio."

My mum shuddered.

"We saw some of them. People staggering around, blood soaking their clothes, some lying in the street. And the sound of people screaming. Screaming and screaming. I'll never forget it, not till the day I die."

"Still, you're home now, thanks be to God," my granny said. "That's the main thing."

"It was a nightmare getting home, wasn't it, Victor?"

"Chaos!" he said. "Sheer unadulterated chaos. The police would send you one way and then the other. It's taken us more than two hours."

My granda switched the radio on again. More news was filtering through: four believed dead in a bomb at Oxford Street station, more fatalities at Cave Hill. There were also reports of an exodus from the city, and heavy queues on all routes out. My dad decided to wait a while before setting off.

It meant that we were still at my granda's when the evening news came on the television. I still remember the pictures of the bombs exploding, the burning buildings, the injured people. But most of all the police trying to clear up afterwards, scraping blood and guts off what was left of Oxford Street Bus Station with shovels and gloved hands, sealing up bits of bodies in clear plastic evidence bags.

Chapter 4

My Mother's Kitchen

IN JANUARY 1970, the local primary school, the D.H. Christie Memorial, opened its new reception class for four-year-olds, following a campaign led by my mum. My brother and sister were already at the Christie, and I was looking forward to going too. I could read, write my name and count to ten, and I wanted to learn more.

But most of all I hoped to find a friend. I'd only my mum to play with at home, and most of the time she'd be getting on with the housework. On Monday mornings we'd wash the clothes. I'd keep her company while she got on with the work of scrubbing the clothes against a washing board, rinsing them, squeezing out the water with the mangle, and finally hanging them to dry in the garden or on the clothes horse near the electric fire, depending on the weather.

We often had the radio on as we worked. I loved it when "Two Little Boys" by Rolf Harris came on. We'd sing along, sometimes even with actions—me falling to the ground and my mother galloping over to save me.

But I was getting fed up with chores and was desperate to start school. It was only for a couple of hours the first few days, to help us settle in. My mum came to pick me up on the first day.

"So tell me all about it," she said. "Did you have a good time?"

I shook my head, tears misting behind my eyes.

"Oh, darling, don't cry," she said, kneeling down and pulling me into a hug.

"I was so looking forward to it," I whispered. "But I didn't like it, Mummy."

"So tell me what happened?"

"We didn't do any learning," I said. "None at all. Just played the whole time."

"Well, that sounds like fun," she said.

"It was, for the boys. They got to play with the water tray and the sand. The girls played in the Wendy house."

"And didn't you enjoy that?"

"No. I hate Wendy houses. They're stupid. And the other girls don't like me."

By this time we were home.

"I'll tell you what," Mummy said. "Let's do some baking. There's just about time before your dad gets home for lunch."

I loved baking with my mother—fruit squares, shortbread, coconut haystacks, apple tarts, rock buns, scones, soda bread… She started to wash down the surfaces while I fetched the margarine, eggs and milk from the fridge. Then I dragged a chair over to the long counter and clambered on top of it.

"What are we going to make?" I asked.

"Apple tart, I think. Right. I'll need 14 ounces of flour."

I loved measuring out the ingredients for her.

"Plain or self-raising?" I asked.

"Plain, please."

I tipped the flour into the mixing bowl as my mother got

on with coring and peeling the apples. As the apples stewed, she started to make the pastry, rubbing the margarine into the flour, then adding sugar and an egg yolk.

"It's nearly done. Time for your special touch," she said and slid the bowl over to me for the final squeeze and turn. I passed the bowl back. My mum divided the dough, then rolled out the first piece of pastry. She eased it onto a greased Pyrex plate.

"Do you want to help me with the apple?" she said.

I nodded. She gave me the spoon, then guided my hand into the saucepan, helped me scoop up some apple and deposit it on top of the pastry, then back to the saucepan.

"That's great," she said.

"Now for the lid." She rolled out the other lump of pastry and laid it over the apple. Soon it was in the oven.

"Oh look, there's a bit left over. Do you want to make something with it?"

I took the pastry and rolled it and rolled it and then reformed it into a lump and rolled it again. Finally I spooned jam, some leftover apple and a few sultanas into the middle of it. Then I folded the pastry over, and my mum helped me seal the edge and mark a C with the knife on top before placing it on a baking tray and popping it into the oven.

The kitchen was warm and delicious. We tidied up while we waited for the oven to complete the job. My mother was never a tidy worker, and the debris of our efforts was strewn across every surface. I put away what I could while my mum removed the rolling pin, wooden spoons, knives and pots to the sink for washing. By the time she had washed up and was wiping down the surfaces, the apple tart was ready to come out of the oven.

"Oh, it smells good," my mum said. "We'll have it after dinner with some ice cream. Your dad will be home soon—I'll just put the stew on to heat through, then we'll go and sit down for five minutes."

I took my orange juice through to the living room. My mum followed with her coffee.

"You know, Constance," she said, "you've got to give school a chance."

"I don't need school. I've got you. I want to stay at home."

"Oh, darling, it's only the first day. It'll get better. Just you wait and see. You've got to give it another try."

I wasn't convinced, but next day I was back at the Christie. There were new children starting who'd not been there the day before. One of them was holding on to her mother. She had short, straight, dark hair and huge brown eyes, full of tears. I went up to her. "Do you want to see the Wendy house?"

She looked up and nodded. She followed me across the room, and soon we were playing together. Her name was Clare Lecky, and from that day on she was my best friend. She lived just up the road. We would sit on the swing at her house and sing:

> I want my tea at McCullaghs' house
> I want my tea at Leckys' house
> I want my tea at McCullaghs' house
> I want my tea at Leckys' house.

Over and over, sometimes for an hour or more.

We both went home from school for lunch, walking part of the way together, me turning off at Cairnvale Avenue while Clare carried on along the Ballycairn Road. One day, a couple of months after I started school, I arrived home for lunch as usual, but when I knocked on the door there was no answer. I pushed open the letter-box.

"Mummy," I shouted. "It's me. I'm here."

Still no answer. I squinted through the letter-box—six feet of patterned carpet and the bottom half of the walls told me nothing. But I could smell burning.

"Mummy? Mummy? Are you OK?"

I'd seen Lassie rescuing someone from a burning building the week before, dragging them to safety through the smoke and the flames. What if my mum needed rescuing?

I ran down the garden path then turned to look back at the house. No sign of flames or smoke. I dashed round to the back of the house. Again, nothing. I started to calm down. Maybe I'd imagined the burning smell.

I went back to the letter-box. Still the burning smell. I sat down on the front step, puzzled. And then I realised what it was. The dinner.

Before I'd started school, she'd often leave the dinner on low while we went to the shops. It was more than a mile each way, and if it took longer to get the messages than she'd expected, sometimes the dinner would start to burn. It was probably the same story today. I'd just have to pass the time until she got back from the shops.

I decided to count how many windows we had. I walked a little way down the front path so that I could look up at the front of the house, but what caught my eye was the name plate: "Vicsie," it said. It was named after my parents, the "Vic" coming from the first three letters of my father's name, Victor, and the "sie" from the last three of my mother's name, Maisie. I stared at Vicsie while I waited for my mum to arrive home, trying to make up different words from the letters. It was a game my granda had taught me, but Vicsie was a tricky set of letters.

"Is" came quickly, followed by "ice".

But it was a few minutes before I saw "vice"—the benefits of weekly Sunday school. I continued to stare.

"Vices."

"Constance! Constance!" I turned to see my mother panting up the hill, laden with shopping bags. She broke into a run in the drive before halting at the door. She began searching through her bag for the key.

"Hello, love. We won't be a minute," she said. "Sorry I'm late. I got held up."

"The dinner's burning."

"Oh no. Where in the name of God is that key?"

She finally located it in her coat pocket and fumbled it into the lock. She burst through the front door and straight into the kitchen. A great hiss erupted as she stuck the burning dinner under the cold tap.

I started to ferry the bags into the house, one at a time.

"Oh, thanks, darling. You're the only bright spot in my day. Now what am I going to do with this mince?" She decanted the least burnt bits into a fresh saucepan.

"That'll do your father. Now what can I give you?"

I held out for toast followed by creamed rice sprinkled with currants—a flies' graveyard my mum called it. I sat at the table eating while my mum got on with scouring the burnt saucepan, wanting to hide the evidence before my father got home just after one.

I made sure I was gone by then. Leaving while it was still my mother's kitchen.

Chapter 5

My Father's Kitchen

I HATED FAMILY meal times. My father's temper held us all in terror. You were never sure if there was going to be an explosion and who would get hurt. Little things would enrage him.

"Joanna, you've set the bloody table wrong. Again. Are you bloody stupid or what?"

Joanna would scurry around swapping the knives and forks over in a panic. She often put the knives where the forks should go, the forks where the knives should go. It was because she was left-handed.

"S-s-sorry," she'd stammer.

If we were lucky, it would be a passing cloud, occasional jibes the worst we had to suffer. But on a bad day his voice would rock the kitchen, angry insults spat at whoever he felt had crossed him. Most often it was my mother.

"You call that a meal for a working man. Do you? Do you call that fucking plate a meal for a working man? The kids have got as much as I have. Do you think that would fucking fill me? Do you? Do you?"

His voice would rise higher and higher, filling the kitchen, till he'd climax by smashing a plate or slamming his way out of the house, banging the kitchen and front doors behind him.

Afterwards my mother would say, "Finish up your tea, children. Then you can go and play for half an hour." She would never make any reference to the scene that had just happened. Not even when he beat us for breaking the sunbed.

It was May 1973. I was seven, my sister ten, my brother thirteen. My mother had gone back to work the previous September, as a shop assistant in the local department store, Dixon's of Coleraine. She started part-time, finishing at 2.30 so she could be home for when I got back from school. But after Easter she went full-time. It meant that the house was empty when I got home. I'd let myself in with the back-door key, which lived under a tin of paint in the garage. I would help myself to some juice and whatever baking was in the cupboard—caramel shortbread or rock cakes or fruit squares. Then I'd get changed and go round to Clare's till teatime.

But on this particular day in May, Clare was off to the dentist's after school, so I decided to play in our back garden for a while. It was a rare sunny day and I was dressed in shorts and a T-shirt rather than my usual navy tracksuit. I was practising handstands, concentrating on staying upside down for as long as possible, when a jet of something cold and wet hit me in the stomach. I looked around for the source of attack.

Splatt.

Another jet of cold water hit me in the face. This time I could see my foe. Katy Bradley, my back-door neighbour, was grinning across the fence at me, a fluorescent yellow water pistol in her hand.

"Do you want to come and play water pistols in my garden this afternoon?" she asked.

"Mine's broken," I lied. I didn't have one. I was struck by

sudden inspiration. "But I could use one of the empty washing-up bottles I've been saving for school."

Five minutes later I was playing water pistols around the Bradley's garden, Katy and me against her brother and sister. It was great fun, creeping up on each other round corners, hiding behind walls to launch our ambushes. My washing-up bottle was a great success—more powerful than their flimsy toys.

At four o'clock the Bradleys went in for their afternoon sweetie time, and I popped back over the fence to get a drink at home and to refill my empty washing-up bottle. It was my big mistake. While I'd been playing at the Bradleys', my sister had also been busy. With the help of Gary McCauley, who lived round the corner, Joanna had put up my mother's brand new sunbed in the back garden. Nobody had actually told us not to touch it, but the sight of the sunbed made me nervous.

As I walked towards the back door, I passed within a few feet of it.

"You'd better not spray that water at me," said Gary.

"Why, what'll you do about it?"

In answer he rushed over to me and pushed me, hard. Taken by surprise, I fell backwards, arms flailing, before landing, inevitably, on the sunbed. There was a loud crack as it gave way beneath me.

Please, please, please, don't let it be broken.

But it was. I picked myself up, trembling with fear.

"You stupid little bastard," I screamed at Gary. "You brainless little git."

My sister, who'd been inside getting some biscuits, came back out when she heard me shouting. "L-look what you've done. You've b-broken M-Mummy's sunbed. He'll k-k-kill us, if he f-finds out," she said.

"It's not my fault. He pushed me. Anyway, I didn't bring it out in the first place."

We worked at the sunbed for ages, panicky fingers trying to push and pull it back into shape. But the leg had twisted and buckled. It was beyond us to repair it.

"M-maybe we could just p-put it away," Joanna said. "Hope n-no-one finds out it was us."

But the angle of the broken leg meant we couldn't fold it away again. It was no use. We were going to be caught. It was now 4.45. There was nothing we could do but wait for my parents to get home from work. It was a long slow hour as we sat in the garden. Not speaking. Not even panicking now. Just awaiting our fate.

At 5.45 the car drew up at the front of the house. We heard the front door slam, then saw my mother in the kitchen, which overlooked the garden. My father was nowhere in sight.

Seeing us through the window, my mother came out into the garden.

"What are you two looking so glum about?"

Before we could answer, her eye moved on to the sunbed.

"What's that doing out here?" she said. "And what's happened to it?"

"It wasn't my fault," I said. "I just came home for a drink and Gary McCauley pushed me and I fell and I landed on the sunbed and it broke and it wasn't my fault."

"What was it doing out in the first place?"

"I b-brought it out. I d-didn't think you'd m-mind. I'm s-sorry it's broken."

"Are you going to tell Dad?" I said, tears starting to spill out of my eyes.

"I'm going to have to tell him. He's going to want to know how the new sunbed got broken."

"Couldn't you say you did it? Please, Mummy. Please."

She turned away from us and went back into the house. My sister and I stayed outside. Sitting a little way apart. Our brief hope crushed. At least the punishment would be over soon.

Then splitting the evening air, my father's voice: "They've done what! They'll be fucking sorry. The little shits."

The kitchen door slammed. My sister and I tensed. He'd come and get us now. But he didn't. There was a pause, then I heard him open the garage door at the front of the house.

"What's he doing? Why's he not coming?" I whispered to my sister.

"I d-don't know."

Five minutes later my mum called us in to set the table for tea. Near the kitchen door stood a stick, long and thick and rough. I'd not seen it before, certainly not in the kitchen. A single sob escaped from me.

"What's going to happen?" I asked my mother. But she didn't answer, wouldn't look at us.

In silence we got out the blue metal picnic table that served as our dining table. We placed a chair along each of the four sides and a stool for me, the youngest, at the corner between my brother and sister.

Then we laid the table. My sister, nervous, got the knives and forks the wrong way round, so I went behind her correcting them. We placed the ketchup, vinegar, salt and pepper in the middle, along with a plate of buttered white bread. My mother put the food on the plates and then put a plate in each of the five places. She called my brother and father to come for their tea. All five of us sat down round the table and began to eat. My brother chatted briefly to my father about cricket, but soon he fell quiet. We ate in silence.

I didn't feel like eating. Could barely chew. But I knew I'd get in more trouble if I didn't eat my food, so I forced down my fish fingers, swallowing somehow as my throat contracted with fear.

After tea Simon excused himself from the table. My sister and I remained. As usual we helped my mother clear up. We moved the dishes to the sink. All the time I could feel my father's eyes watching me, but I did not dare look at him.

We moved all of the chairs but his back against the wall. Still he sat looking at us. Eventually he got up and moved his own chair. Then he pushed the table against the wall.

"You can leave this to me now, Maisie," he said.

"Victor…" she started to say but he cut her off. "Just go," he said. My mother left the room.

"Your mother's told me about the trouble you've caused today."

"It wasn't …" I started to say.

"Shut, the fuck, up." He spat the words into my face. "I am not interested in your snivelling little excuses.

"Joanna, go over to the table and lean against it with your back to me."

My sister didn't move.

"Now," he screamed.

She scurried to the table. I could see her shaking as she stretched her hands out to grip its cold blue edge. I watched him pick up the stick and move to stand a couple of paces behind my sister. He licked his lips and seemed to smile to himself.

Then he stepped towards her whilst swinging the stick. As the blow landed on my sister's bare legs he said, "Don't."

He stepped back and then swung again.

"Ever."

And again.

"Take."

And again.

"Things."

Another blow.

"That don't."

And another.

"Belong."

And a last.

"To you.

"Now get upstairs to your bed."

My sister limped from the kitchen, shutting the door behind her. It was my turn. I took up the position without waiting for him to ask. He repeated the ritual, the words slightly different.

"Don't.

"Ever.

"Break.

"Other.

"People's.

"Things."

The pain was red hot on my bare legs. His full weight transmitted through the stick. It was hard to keep my balance against the force. Snot and tears splashed on to the table as each blow landed.

"Now get out of my sight."

I followed my sister up to bed. It was difficult climbing the stairs, large red welts already raised on both my legs from the top of my thighs to just above my knees.

Downstairs the front door slammed, my father off out for the night. When she was sure he'd gone, my mother came up to our bedroom. We were both lying face down on our bed. I heard her gasp as she caught sight of our legs, striped with red, dotted with dark splinters from the rough old piece of wood.

Then in a cheery voice: "Your father's gone out. I thought you might come down and watch TV. *Top of the Pops* is on later."

I turned my tear-stained face to look at her. She looked away.

"We'll make some supper and get ourselves comfy on the sofa. OK? I'll be back in a minute."

She returned with some warm salty water. We lay on the bed as she gently bathed our wounds. We didn't say anything and neither did she. There was nothing to be said.

Chapter 6

Turning Point

THE SUMMER OF '73 was a turning point in my life. For the first time my mother was not at home for the long summer holidays. I was free to do whatever I wanted. Well, largely free. I had to be home for dinner with my dad, and I wasn't allowed to go downtown. The whole of Northern Ireland was exploding, but it wasn't until Coleraine was bombed that my parents decided that the centre of town wasn't safe for a seven-year-old girl.

I was at school when Coleraine was hit, just before 3 p.m. on Tuesday, 12 June. We were reading when an explosion cut through the quiet. From nearby came the tinkling of breaking glass.

"Miss, was that the quarry? It sounded loud. Miss, I think that was a bomb."

"Shhh now, Ray. Get on with your book," our teacher, Mrs McCracken, said.

"But, Miss. What was it? Was it a bomb?" There was fear in his voice. His uncle had been one of the Bloody Friday dead.

"It was probably just the quarry. Now settle back down. It's not long till home time."

But the sound hadn't come from that direction. And if it was the quarry, why had the siren summoning the part-time firemen started to wail? Even so, I settled back down. Reading was always a pleasure. My mind went back to the book in front of me.

Booommmmm!!!!

Another great blast sounded out from across the river. Ray was out of his seat.

"Oh, Miss, that was a bomb. That was definitely a bomb. Oh, no. Oh, no."

Others were joining in.

"Where was it?"

"Is there going to be any more?"

"I'm scared, Miss."

Mrs McCracken took charge.

"Enough now, children. There's nothing can be achieved by you worrying. Now pack your bags and then put your heads on the desk."

"But, Miss."

"That's enough now. Another word and you'll feel my cane."

We got on with tidying away our things, but there was tension in the room, waiting for another explosion.

My parents both worked in the centre of town. I hoped they were OK.

At five past three the bell went. I picked my coat up from the cloakroom and then made my way quickly home. As soon as I got there I phoned my mother's work. 2-7-6-2. But I couldn't get through. I switched on the radio. It was tuned to Radio Ulster.

"This is a newsflash. Reports are coming in of two explosions in the centre of Coleraine."

My sister arrived home and we waited together for news.

Radio Ulster was just reporting that "Four are feared dead in Coleraine bombing," when I saw my mother hurrying up the drive.

"Were the bombs near you, Mummy?"

She nodded. "Quite near. One was at the top of Railway Road, the other at Stewart's Garage, you know, at Hanover Place. It's a complete wreck."

"They say there's people dead. I heard it on the radio."

"I don't know."

"Is Daddy all right?"

"I'm sure he is."

A few minutes later Simon arrived home from school, but it was another twenty before my dad appeared, unscathed. It was Coleraine's turn to be on the news that night. Six dead. More than thirty injured. Three had lost limbs.

So it wasn't a surprise that the centre of town was out of bounds that summer. I didn't mind; I'd plenty to do playing, riding my bike and watching TV. I'd get up when I wanted, after my parents had gone to work, make my own breakfast and eat it in front of children's TV. *Robinson Crusoe*, the *Banana Splits*, Laurel and Hardy: hours of happy viewing lay before me.

The mornings were for TV, the afternoons for playing. At the bottom of our road lay the playing fields of the boys' grammar school, the Inst. They were protected by a large green fence, topped with barbed wire and signs declaring "Property of Coleraine Academical Institution. Trespassers Prosecuted". Like everyone else, I ignored them, slipping through a hole in the fence cut by one of the older boys. I'd play on the Tarzan swing at the edge of the big forest, or football if there were other kids around. But most of all I liked to escape into the countryside on my blue and gold Kingpin bike, my best ever birthday present from the year before. I loved cycling up to the mound, an old Norman fort about half a mile's ride from our house. You could see right down the river as far as the sea at Castlerock from the top of the mound, then cycle past fields of potatoes and cows to the main road and a fast descent downhill back towards home.

I loved my summer days. Except for dinner time when my father came home. I had to be careful then. My father's use of my child body was infrequent, limited to the rare occasions when we were alone. But he had moved on from poking his dirty fingers inside me while touching himself to having me touch him. He had taught me how to rub my hand up and down him, while he got harder and stiffer, his face contorting, his breath gasping, till he erupted, wet and sticky.

I'd learned to focus on the task in hand, keeping the rhythm steady, not gripping too tightly, not going too fast. If a job's worth doing . . . And I knew that if I failed by hand, I'd end up with his penis in my mouth, thrusting and forcing, suffocating and choking me. Then he'd spurt into my mouth and I'd have to swallow it down, holding back vomit as well as tears.

So as far as possible I avoided being on my own with him. But one Tuesday, at the beginning of August, I failed to follow my golden rule. My dad had arrived home at one o'clock as usual for dinner with me, my brother and my sister. Afterwards, Joanna and Simon went straight out to see their friends, but I decided to take my frisbee round to Clare's to play with that afternoon.

I was in my bedroom searching for it when my father came in behind me and shut the door. I pretended not to notice him, hoping he'd go away, and carried on with my searching.

"What are you looking for?" he asked.

"My powerball." (I'd found the frisbee soon after he came in, but had not wanted to stop searching while he was still in the room.)

"Here, I'll help you."

My father usually spent his time shouting and complaining about my toys. Rather than helping me find anything, he usually wanted to throw my things away. I stepped back and he bent down to search in the cupboard. He quickly found my multi-coloured ball and stood up with it in his hand.

"Here it is," he said, handing it over to me.

I took it, thanking him as I shoved it in my tracksuit pocket and made to leave the room.

"I think I deserve a bit more thanks than that," he said as he nipped in between me and the door.

He started to unzip his fly.

"I don't want to," I muttered.

"What was that you said?" His voice rising.

"I don't want to," I said again. "I'm going to be late for Clare."

I don't know why I answered him back. I never answered him back. It never did me any good to answer him back.

"You're not going anywhere," he said.

He grabbed my arm and threw me on to the bed, face down. Quickly he came behind me and started to pull down my tracksuit bottoms and my pants. I could feel him fumbling inside his trunks with his other hand.

I was not prepared for the pain that seared through me as he forced himself inside me. Faster and faster he thrust, pounding into my body. Pain took hold of every inch of me. Then the tell-tale exclamation.

As he zipped himself up he said, "You're an evil child, rotten to the core. That's why this has to happen. Because you are so bad. And I'm going to fuck that badness out of you if it's the last thing I do."

With that he left me lying on the bed, his sperm and my blood mixing together down my leg.

I didn't go to Clare's that afternoon, called her up to say I didn't feel well. Instead I stayed at home and thought about what had happened, what he'd said. At last it was clear what I had to do to stop it happening. If my dad abused me because I was bad, then all I needed to do to stop the abuse was become good. At everything. It was that simple.

Chapter 7

Hallowe'en's Coming

A COUPLE OF weeks before my eighth birthday in September 1973, my mum asked me if I wanted to have a party.

"I'd love a party," I replied. "But could I wait and have it at Hallowe'en?"

"Oh, Constance, I'm not sure about that."

"Please, Mummy. Please. You know how much I love Hallowe'en."

And it was true. I did. Hallowe'en and everything to do with it: witches, broomsticks, toffee apples, nuts. In the end she gave in.

I prepared the invitations myself—pieces of plain white card, carefully covered with drawings of bats and ghosts, witches' hats and skeletons.

YOU ARE INVITED TO A HALLOWE'EN PARTY ON 31ST OCTOBER
at 6.30PM AT 13 CAIRNVALE AVENUE.
PLEASE COME IN FANCY DRESS.

I made lists of things to eat and games to play: bobbing for apples and monkey nuts, biting an apple suspended on a string without using your hands and Hallowe'en hunt the spider, with a black plastic spider I bought with my pocket money. I even wrote out copies of a Hallowe'en song for everyone:

Hallowe'en's coming, Hallowe'en's coming,
Skeletons will be after you!
Witches, cats and big black bats,
Ghosts and goblins too-oo,
Ghosts and goblins too.

A few days beforehand, my mum and I prepared the turnip lanterns which would be the focus of the decorations—slicing off the tops to make lids, hollowing out the insides and carving them into scary faces. Then my mum made a little hole in the bottom of each one, filled it with melted wax and planted a candle firmly in the middle of it. I stayed well back for this part. I'd set myself alight the previous year when the sleeve of my witch's gown wafted into my lantern as I tried to secure the candle in an upright position.

Luckily I was in the kitchen at the time and had enough wit to stick my arm into the sink and turn the tap on full blast. The flames went out quickly, but the arm of the cloak and my anorak beneath were both burned. I'd had the anorak for only a few weeks, and my father was none too impressed.

But I had no hesitation about making the very same gown a central feature of my Hallowe'en party costume. My mother had agreed to repair it, and I knew that once I put it together with a witch's mask and a hat, I'd look fantastic.

It wasn't till a couple of days before the party that my confidence began to falter. My mum still hadn't fixed the gown, and she'd not got me a mask either. The hat I'd saved from the year before. It was black cardboard with an orange and black checked rim. As witches' hats go it wasn't bad but far from enough on its own.

That night I reminded my mum about my outfit.

"I'll make sure to look it out tonight," she promised. But Mrs Wallace dropped in so she didn't get the time.

The outfit preyed on my mind all day at school. As soon as tea was finished I raised it again.

"Don't worry, Constance," she said. "I haven't forgotten. I'll sort it out tonight, should I be up till four in the morning to do it." She gave me a hug. "Come on, let's go and get it out now."

We went into the living room and she opened up the mahogany-stained cabinet where she stored material, wool, patterns, recipes, knitting needles and God alone knew what else. She called it Pandora's Box as she was never sure what would emerge when she opened the doors.

As usual, half the contents spewed forth on to the floor as she released the catch. They were usually stored under pressure, my mother piling and pushing them into the cabinet and then forcing the door shut with her foot.

"Now where did I put that black lining?" she muttered to herself, trailing more and more scraps of material and reams of fabric out of the cabinet and strewing them around her. "I'm sure it was in here." Within a couple of minutes she'd located the intact lining of an old skirt, though it was no longer living with the skirt itself.

The repair material turned out to be the easy part, because hunt as we did, neither I nor my mother could find hide nor hair of the black gown. I went to bed worrying.

"I'm sure I'll find it," my mother said. "I'll have another look after I've made the things for the party. We've already got the hat, and then all you'll need is the mask. Sure I'll get you that in the town tomorrow."

I fell asleep hoping for the sound of the sewing machine, which would signal the unearthing of the gown.

School was closed for Hallowe'en the next day, but I got up early, hoping for good news. My mum was in the kitchen, having her breakfast.

"Hello, dote," she said.

"Have a look in the fridge," she went on. "You'll see the sausage rolls and cheese and pineapple sticks and cocktail sausages that I made last night for the party."

I knew she'd not found it—we weren't usually allowed to see the food before the party. But still, I had to ask.

"Did you find the gown?"

"No. I think we must've thrown it out last year. It must've been too badly damaged."

I bit down on my bottom lip, not saying anything.

"But sure you'll be fine with a hat and a mask."

I must have looked disappointed because she added, "If I'm back in time I'll try and turn that black lining we found into some sort of cloak."

"Thanks, Mum," I said, briefly relieved. "And thanks for making the food. It looks great."

I was still putting on a brave face when she set off for work. But by dinner time anxiety was eating me alive. I'd been round to see Clare in the morning, her mum cross-questioning me about preparations for the party and what I was going to wear. Clare's outfit had been ready for more than a week.

I went down to the fields at the bottom of the road after dinner, climbing up the rugby posts to sit on the crossbar. From here I would be able to see when my dad left for work. I always liked it sitting on the rugby bar, being up above every-one else. But today I was tormented by my lack of a costume. It was going to be another disaster. Why had I suggested fancy dress? I should have known better. The summer before, my mum had encouraged me to enter a fancy dress competition, promising that she'd come up with a marvellous costume. It turned out to be a disc of cardboard, covered in the gold tin-foil from a Caramac, hung on a piece of red ribbon and worn round my neck over my regulation navy tracksuit. I had a sign, also in cardboard, saying "Mary Peters, Golden Girl", which was all very well but my hair was dark brown.

I felt bad enough as I left our holiday caravan in my non-fancy dress, but when I arrived at the hall where they were judging the competition to behold a Little Bo Peep complete with staff, Batman, Tweedle Dee and Tweedle Dum, a cowgirl and a policeman, I wanted to crawl away and die. But that would have meant hurting my mum's feelings, so I stuck it out. I was not a winner.

Sitting on the rugby posts, I was getting more and more agitated. How could I have been so stupid as to suggest fancy dress? I should have known that it would be like this. In the end I couldn't stand it any more. I decided to do something.

I'd seen my dad go by in the car. I slid down the rugby post and made my way back home.

I reckoned the cloak would be difficult and thought it would be best to get it out of the way first. I dragged the little table over to the fire. It left my mum's overstuffed magazine rack exposed. Then I fetched the black skirt lining and my mum's dressmaking scissors and placed them on the table. Finally I moved the mustard pouffe directly in front of the fire.

I sat down on the pouffe wondering where to begin. I was a little bit daunted. Although I'd watched my mother dress-making many times, I'd no direct experience of my own. I turned the material over a few times, hoping to uncover a point of attack. Nothing revealed itself.

I sat for a few minutes staring at it. Then I picked the material up and went upstairs. My mother's dressing table had three mirrors set at different angles. I hung the black skirt lining down my back, holding it with both hands at my shoulders, and contemplated my reflections. The skirt was quite long, hanging down almost to my knees. It was the perfect length for a cloak. The width wasn't too bad either—perhaps a bit too big for my shoulders but not outrageously so.

The real problem was that it looked quite obviously like a skirt lining—it had seams, a double layer of fabric and, worst of all, a gap where the zip had been.

I decided to make a single layer from the front panel thus eliminating the zip problem. I'd seen my mother unpicking seams. It had always looked fairly easy, and so I found it, once I got the first few stitches undone. It wasn't long before the front panel was free from the rest. Things were going my way.

I snipped off a few loose threads and then hung it from my shoulders. It was definitely looking better, though it was a shame that it had lined a fairly straight skirt. It was only a little wider at the bottom than the top and didn't have the billowing effect I would have wanted. Still, at this stage, I'd no room to be fussy.

The next bit was the most tricky. I couldn't be holding on to the cloak with my hands all night. I needed to be able to fasten it at the neck. After several attempts I managed to cut two strips from the black material to make the ties. They were a bit raggedy and not quite the same length or width, but I reckoned they'd look fine once they were fastened. Now all I had to do was attach them to the gown and I'd be finished. I went back downstairs and got out a needle and some black thread. I'd started embroidery at school the previous year and knew enough to make a reasonable job of sewing on the ties.

I put the cloak on and then returned to my mother's mirrors. It looked pretty good. Now all I needed was a mask. We'd made some at school, but they were hanging up in the classroom. Still, if I'd been able to make one once, I was sure I could do it again.

From my bedroom I fetched the white card left over from the invitations, along with felt pens, crayons and colouring pencils. I started by cutting a large oval piece of card. Well, at least I was trying for oval though it was a bit rough looking in places. I decided the face should be green, but after several unsuccessful searches through my pencil case for the green pencil, I opted for blue. My arm was frenzied, turning the big white card blue, but inside the anxiety had almost gone.

Next I tried to draw in eyes, a nose and a mouth, but it was hard to see them through the strong blue background.

"Ahhh!!!" I screamed in frustration, wanting to rip it up. But there wasn't enough card to make another, so I settled with banging my fist a few times on the table.

I tried to calm myself and work out what to do now. I decided to start again on the other side, but this time I started by drawing the features in. I coloured in big sneering black lips with a black felt pen which I had to keep licking to get to work, an orange nose covered in purple warts and finally red devil eyes. Even on the white background it looked pretty scary to me.

I dotted a few more purple warts about the chin before returning to the blue colouring pencil to fill in the background.

I was nearly finished. I carefully made a hole on either side of the mask and threaded through some white elastic, knotting it to hold it secure. Then I sat back and looked at my creation.

"Not bad," I thought. "Not bad at all."

Of course, it was nowhere near as good as a shop-bought one. But still, for handmade it was the best I'd seen. But when I slipped it on to see it in action, I discovered that I couldn't see where I was going. I took it off and cut out the middle of my scary red eyes. I returned the mask to my face. I still couldn't see anything. The position of the eyes on the mask in no way corresponded to the position of the eyes on my face.

I pulled the mask away from my face until I could see the holes and then repositioned it so that they were near my eyes. I could see a little bit through the right hole. I squinted at the mirror. The eyes were too high up, and in order to see through even one hole, I had to pull the mask down, exposing part of my forehead and placing the black lips well below my chin.

I tore the mask from my face and threw it down on the floor. "You stupid, stupid, stupid mask," I screamed. "I hate you."

"What's going on, Constance?" It was my mother's voice. I hadn't noticed her come in. "What's wrong?"

"It's that stupid mask," I said, pointing at it. "I made it for tonight, but it's useless. Completely useless."

"Calm down. I've got you a mask. I told you I would. Here it is."

Relief spread throughout my body and a smile settled on my mouth as my mother riffled through her bags before handing me one. I looked inside. A mask stared back at me. But instead of the hooked nose, warts and purple lips I'd been expecting were dark hollow eyes and nose and evenly spaced teeth set in a ghostly white. It wasn't a witch's mask she'd bought me—it was a skeleton's.

"It's not a witch," I said, my voice dull and quiet.

"No, they'd none left. I got this instead. Try it on. It'll be just as good."

Just as good! Just as good! How could it be just as good? This wasn't enough for an outfit. It was just a mask. The wrong mask.

"But I'm going as a witch. I've got the hat, I made the cloak myself today. All I needed was the mask."

I turned from her and ran up the stairs as fast as I could. I went into my bedroom and slammed the door behind me. I could hear my mother coming up the stairs. "Constance," she was calling. "Constance, come here."

But I didn't want to. I wanted to get away. Away from this house. Away from this family. I ran to the window, pulled it open. I was clambering on to the sill, ready to jump out when my mother's arms swept me up from behind. I struggled for a moment, then went limp. My mother shut the window and laid me on the bed.

"Constance. Constance. What were you doing?"

I didn't speak.

"Come on now, darling. Nothing's this bad. Why are you in such a state?"

I lay there silent.

"Listen, the party's going to be great. There's enough food to feed an army. I was up till past midnight getting it ready. You'll have a good time, all the party games we've sorted out and the lanterns and the song. And you're going to look great. Did I hear you say that you'd made a cloak?"

I nodded.

"Well done. Will you show me it?"

I gestured vaguely with my hand towards the wardrobe where I'd hung it up with such pride earlier that afternoon. My mum walked over to it. "Do you mean in here?"

I nodded again.

She opened up the wardrobe and took out the cloak.

"This is really good, Constance. It'll go really well with the skeleton mask. The man in the shop told me they've been selling like hot cakes."

I didn't have the strength to argue. Whoever heard of a skeleton wearing a cloak? Or a witch's hat?

"I'll just go and get it for you. I'll be back in a minute," she said. "Will you be OK?"

I nodded.

"You won't do anything silly, will you?"

"No," I said.

She was back in a minute. "There you go," she said. "Why don't you get yourself ready while I put the food out downstairs?"

I lay on the bed for a while after she'd gone, not really thinking about anything. If I could, I would have stayed there all evening. But I knew I had to get up; my friends would be coming soon. I got up slowly and changed into black trousers and a black jumper. Then I put on the mask and fastened the cloak around my neck. I deliberately kept away from the mirrors. No point upsetting myself.

I was just putting on my shoes when the doorbell rang. It was Clare, a little early, looking fantastic as Peter Pan.

"Is that what you're wearing?" she said. "What are you supposed to be?"

I spotted the witch's hat out of the corner of my eye, a plan forming in my mind. I put it on.

"I'm a witch's skeleton."

Chapter 8

Barking Mad

"SIT! STAND!! DOWN!"

It was Easter Monday and my dad was on the beach in Portrush, shouting commands at our golden Labrador, Goldie. My mum and I were sitting on a bench on the promenade above, eating ice cream. As a treat my mum had bought me a 99. I pushed the flake down the middle of the cone, bit off the end and sucked the ice cream through it.

"What, in the name of God, does he look like?" my mother said. She shook her head.

I looked down at him. He was wearing what he considered to be the correct outfit for dog training: brown suede desert boots, old faded pink cords, a green parka and a brown cap. I'm not sure how the boots, cords and cap made their way into his costume, but the parka was pure Big Sammy.

Big Sammy ran the dog obedience training classes at the Orange Hall in Articlave every Monday evening between seven and nine. His face was a large, somewhat misshapen potato. He was bald and had tight piggy eyes, tiny close-set ears and a wide mouth with large discoloured teeth. The "Big" came not from his height, which was average, but his width. With a huge barrel chest and great thick arms, he was more Big Daddy than Giant Haystacks.

Sammy was a security guard at the canning factory in Coleraine and was in charge of the guard dogs there. Alsatians were his passion, and he would lavish attention on anyone arriving for his obedience training class with one. My dad didn't have an Alsatian, but he was still mesmerised by Big Sammy.

My dad was determined to turn Goldie into an obedience champion and so win favour with the sainted Sammy. Goldie's first obedience show was scheduled for the following Saturday, so there was an added intensity to the sits, downs and stands as my dad put him through his paces on the beach.

"I don't know why he had to practise on *that* beach," my mum said. "Spoiling the day for the people down from Belfast. All we can hope is that nobody knows we're with one man and his dog."

My father had chosen the smallest of Portrush's three beaches for his dog obedience training session. While the east and west strands both stretched away for miles, he'd opted for the tiny fifty-yard strip just below Main Street. Nestled between two outcrops of rock and backed by the prom, it was crowded with families with young children. It was a sunny day but hardly warm. Still, most of the holiday-makers had stripped to T-shirts or swimming costumes. Who knew when a sunny bank holiday would come along again? The rocks were scattered with clothes and bags, rackets and balls, buckets and spades—all the usual accompaniments to a day at the beach. Parents sat on the rocks or lounged against the prom wall, trying to relax while keeping one eye on their children, splashing in and out of the sea, building sandcastles or playing tig.

My father stood among them, Goldie straining for his commands, twenty yards away. He'd already caught a few holidaymakers out, practising walking with dog to heel through the streets of Portrush. This involved sharp turns and stopping abruptly every so often. Goldie would try to sit immediately by his side. He'd learnt from experience that a moment's hesitation resulted in a swift kick to his leg. This would have been bad enough for any dog, but Goldie had a bad hip and a blow to the leg was particularly painful.

Having been through months of training, my mum and I were by now familiar with the sudden stops during the practice of walking with dog to heel and so did not walk too closely behind my father. But one unfortunate child collided with my father's suddenly stationary legs and ended up squashing her ice cream on to her face. Her mother appeared not to be impressed, but from the distance at which we followed, I could not hear her exact words.

Although it would be the first obedience show that we had entered, it was not our first dog show. Goldie had already been a largely unsuccessful show dog. I'd been begging for a pet for years, and my dad had finally relented two years earlier. He decided we should start with two budgies, to be called Jock and Joey. But luckily Aunt Gertrude bought a budgie, so he went for a dog instead.

Goldie had not been bought as a show dog but as a family pet. He did not come from a line of champions. It was only after my success at the Coleraine and District Agricultural Show that my dad got the bug for showing him. The previous year, the school had entered my embroidered place mat in the show, and it had been awarded second place. This year my ribbed bobble hat, knitted from yellow and brown random wool with a chocolate brown bobble and band, would be making its entry in junior knitting.

By 1974 I was obsessed with winning prizes. It was part of my campaign to prove that I was good after all. The school had a list of all classes in the show, and I scanned it for others open to children of my age. The options were limited: embroidery and flower arranging. I hadn't enough time to produce an embroidered piece of the required standard and knew nothing of flower arranging.

It looked like the bobble hat would be my one chance for success until I noticed the pet show at the end of the catalogue. I'd almost missed it as I'd flicked through the livestock categories that were the main event at the Coleraine show. There were not many pet categories, but Goldie and I were eligible for two: junior dog handler and the waggiest tail competition.

The show was held over three damp days in May. My dad had agreed to take Goldie and me to the showgrounds, on the far side of town, in time for my two classes on the Thursday evening.

The junior dog handler was first. We took our place in the ring with an assortment of other children and their dogs: three mongrels, a collie, a poodle, a spaniel, a whippet and two Jack Russells. The judge, a short, fat, tweedy woman, placed us at intervals around the ring and then thundered out her instructions.

"Listen carefully now, children. I want you to walk your dogs around the ring, please. In a clockwise direction. You know, the same direction as the little hand. There's the good children."

We started walking. At the end of the third round, she called us to a halt. It was time for the individual examinations.

I'd read about this in my dog encyclopaedia and was prepared for showing Goldie's teeth. We'd practised at home with some Good Boy drop rewards. The girl before me hadn't prepared so well, crying as her whippet snapped at her hand. After two more circuits of the ring, the judge pulled four children and their dogs forward. I was one of them. We were awarded fourth reserve prize. Not fantastic, but it was better than nothing.

The tail-wagging competition followed. I had high hopes for this one. It was held in the same ring with the same judge and almost all the same entrants. I looked into Goldie's face and said "good boy" in my most enthusiastic voice. His tail started to swish from side to side. I stroked his golden head— "good boy; clever, clever dog"—and the tail picked up momentum. As the judge approached, it was lashing back and forth.

The judging was swift this time—and we won. I received a box of Bonios for Goldie and a tiny cup for myself. I was ecstatic. My father, too, was impressed and a few days later announced his intention to show Goldie.

He entered the next open show. It was in Ballymena, twenty-eight miles away, six weeks later, and was full of all sorts of different breeds: wolfhounds, bloodhounds, corgis, setters, boxers. I was in heaven.

My dad entered two classes: labrador puppy and gundog puppy. He received fourth reserve in the Labrador class. It was the highest placing Goldie ever achieved. Over the next few months, we attended shows all over Northern Ireland— Crumlin, Lisburn, Portadown, Magherafelt—with Goldie appearing under his showname, Golden Wonder. He was placed only one more time—again as fourth reserve.

"Them judges is fools," my father said, as we drove back

from his latest attempt. "Pure fools. Did you see that great heifer that won the day? That's the type that's always winning. Big hefty lumps they are. Our Goldie's too fine boned. He's never going to be a champion, not while they're in charge. There's no point showing him."

"So is that the end of the dog shows?" I asked, trying to keep the disappointment out of my voice. I loved going to the shows, meeting all those dogs.

"I'm not beat yet," he said. "No, I just need a new plan. I'll show those buffoons. It's time to get me a new dog."

And so began a period of extensive research on what type of dog to get and its potential for success. Dalmatians, basenjis, Samoyeds and dachshunds—all were considered and discarded. None of them quite clicked with my dad. And then it came to him. A Scottish dog. That was what he needed. That would feel right.

His focus narrowed to Scottish breeds: West Highland whites, bearded collies, Gordon setters and Scottish terriers were all in the running, but he finally settled on a Shetland sheepdog. There was a breeder, Sandra Scott, not far from Coleraine. And her dogs had champion pedigree.

I went with my father to visit her one Saturday. She lived in an old and draughty house set back from the road on a farm just outside the village of Ballybogy. It was as well she lived out in the country, for the dogs put up a tremendous racket as we approached the house. As we got out of the car, a huge, fluffy, gleaming white dog bounded towards us, followed by a tall, slim woman dressed in wellies, jeans and a jumper.

"Is that a poodle?" I asked her. "I've never seen one so big."

"Aye, she's a standard poodle."

"What's her name? Can I stroke her?"

"Her show name is Ballybogy Snow Queen, but you can call her Queenie. And of course you can stroke her."

"I didn't know you bred poodles," my dad said.

"Poodles, Yorkshire terriers too. But you're after a sheltie, aren't you? Why don't you come in?"

The house was filthy, dog hairs and muddy pawprints covering every inch of surface. Great packs of tripe were thawing in the kitchen. We took a seat in the front room to discuss business.

"Well," she said, "one of my bitches, Ballybogy Dancing Princess, has just come into heat. That's her." She pointed to a photo of a sable sheltie standing next to a large silver cup. "She's a great dog, Irish champion last year. She's being serviced by the Scottish champion, King Callum of Kintyre, on Monday. He's coming over today on the Larne–Stranraer ferry. He's Rob's best dog."

"Rob?" my father asked.

"Rob McGilchrist. He's my fiancé. We met last year at Crufts." She looked down at her lap, suddenly shy.

"Anyway, if all goes well, we'll have pups within ten weeks. But there's five ahead of you on the waiting list. It'll depend on how many she has whether you'll get a pup this time. And as you'll be bottom of the list, you'll get last choice. If you're looking for a show dog, you might want to wait."

But my father didn't do patience, and talk of champion stock and photos of gleaming silverware had him hooked. Sandra agreed to call us once Princess was pregnant. The following week the confirmation call came. And nine weeks later, six pups were born—the sixth a runt, not expected to live. We hoped for the best, but she phoned the next day to say that he'd died.

My father was devastated. But an hour later a second call came. The pup was alive again. Sandra had removed his lifeless body from the litter and set him on top of the washing machine while she got on with feeding the dogs. When she came back to get his little body for burial, he was breathing again. The machine had been through the spin cycle, and she thought this might have restarted his heart.

My mother was all for calling him Lazarus, but my father had already written to Miss MacLeod, owner of the Berwick-upon-Tweed wool shop where my mother bought wool on our Haggerston holidays. Miss MacLeod was a Gaelic speaker and was supplying a list of possible Scottish names for the new dog. My dad chose Aed, meaning blaze, as the pup had a flash of white on his forehead. He decided on a showname of Ballybogy Blazing Light.

We went to pick up Aed when he was twelve weeks old. He was a beautiful little dog, with his fuzzy baby coat and little white paws. "Oh, he's definitely a champion looking at you," my dad said. His only concern was that Aed would be too small, so he gave him a daily supplement of minerals and vitamins called Stress.

At six months Aed was old enough to start showing. His first was one of Ireland's biggest—the Belfast Dog Show at Balmoral showgrounds. It was a championship event, with the chance of winning a challenge certificate; three certificates and Aed would be a champion and could compete at Crufts.

My dad decided that the whole family should attend. He started loading our estate car early on the morning of the show. Dog bowls, brushes, leads, water, food, blankets, *How to Show Your Dog* guide and the *Shetland Sheepdog Handbook* went in first. Goldie was next, behind the restraining bars at the back of the car. Then my mother, brother and sister went into the rear seat. Finally, I took my place in the front seat with Aed on my lap.

Usually my mother was in the front, with Simon, Joanna and me in the back. But I was prone to become car sick. The first time, a few years earlier, I'd thrown up in the back of the car on the motorway travelling into Belfast. My dad had gone berserk. After that I'd been made to sit on a piece of felt-covered hardboard between my parents in the front. I hated sitting there. Not only was it hard and uncomfortable, but I was liable to be slapped and shouted at if I impeded my father's access to the handbrake or gear stick. My mother had then discovered that sucking boiled sweets could help prevent car sickness, so I was allowed to return to the rear with a packet of glacier fruits. I still felt ill, but at least I didn't throw up.

On the day of the show I had too important a function to perform for my father to risk my being sick. I was to spend the journey holding green plasticine on the ends of Aed's ears. My father was convinced that this would ensure that Aed's ears met the breed standard of cocked ears—erect, except for the tip. Aed's ears were properly cocked normally, but my father was taking no risks. Hence me, the dog and the plasticine. He'd considered several substances before deciding on plasticine, which could easily be removed from his fur without leaving any trace.

For once we set off in plenty of time. We needed to arrive at Balmoral by 10.30 a.m. in order to have the dogs registered and kennelled by the cut-off time of 11.00. The first half of the journey went well, and we were past Ballymena by a quarter to nine. Ten minutes later the car screeched to a halt and my dad leaped out shouting, "Get out, get out! It's going to blow."

Smoke was pouring out of the bonnet. My father retreated a further ten yards, leaving us to struggle from the smoking car. Suddenly I realised that Goldie was still in the boot. I dashed back to the car and rescued him. As I returned to my family, my father was in full flow.

"That fucking heap of oul' junk. Them bastards at the garage are for it when I see them. Bloody selling me that fucking shower of shite. They've ruined my chances. Ruined them."

"I'm sure I saw a phone box not that far back," my mother said helpfully. "Why don't you go and phone the AA? I'm sure they'll be able to get us back on the road in no time."

"The AA? The A fucking bastard A? What use will it be to phone them? I'm not in the bloody AA any more. I lapsed the shitting membership last year as I'd never needed to use them. They won't come out if you're not a member. Any more fucking bright suggestions, Brain of Britain?"

My mother sighed and said nothing. At least for a couple of minutes. But then: "Victor, isn't that a breakdown truck coming along the road? Why don't you flag him down and see if he can help?"

In an instant my dad was leaping up and down at the side of the road, flailing his arms about and shouting, "Stop, stop, please stop," at the battered red pickup truck that was approaching on the other side of the road. It slowed down and came to a halt just past our car. Cullybackey Motors was emblazoned on the rear.

The driver of the truck slowly emerged from the vehicle.

He was a young man, in his early twenties, with dark curly hair and a ruddy face, and was dressed in oil-stained blue overalls. The pace of his exit from the truck was nothing compared to his style of conversation. In my experience there are two types of country people: those who speak machine-gun fast like their life depends on reaching the end of the sentence one split second after starting it, and those who talk un-be-lieve-ab-ly slow-ly, en-un-ci-at-ing ev-er-y sin-gle syll-a-ble. Our mechanic was one of the slow ones.

"Were youse, want-ing, an-y ass-ist-ance, at all? With your ve-hic-le? It's look-ing, to me, like it's smok-ing a bit."

Despite his desire to be back on the road, my father could not resist the opportunity to show off his range of accents and immediately adopted the same halting speech as the mechanic.

"We-llll, I was com-ing, round thon cor-ner, back thon-der, when I looked up, and sure, what did I see, but smoke. Smoke, belching out of the motor."

My mother and brother fought to stifle their laughter. My father cut his eye at them before proceeding:

"D'ya think, you can, fix it? We're in, a wee bit, of a hurr-y, you see."

The mechanic may have been slow of speech, but he was swift in his work, and within five minutes of drawing up he'd located the problem (a broken fan belt) and fixed it from a spare he had in his van. If he'd managed to speak a bit quick-er, he'd probably have taken only three.

Soon we were back on the road, and by half nine we were pulling into the car park at Balmoral showgrounds. Even an hour and a half before the kennelling deadline and two before the showing would get under way, Balmoral was already coming to life. There were dogs everywhere, of every shape, size and description, sniffing, peeing and barking or just taking a stroll with their owners. Some I'd seen only in books before: an Italian Spinone, an elegant pharaoh hound and a chow, its shocking thick purple-black tongue hanging out as it lay panting on the grass.

We wandered around for half an hour, taking in the atmosphere and letting the dogs acclimatise. My dad nodded at some of the people he'd met at previous shows. They too came in all shapes and sizes, from the short, chubby Mrs Aitchison with her willowy borzoi to the shuffling Mr McAfee with his pair of Bedlington terriers.

We spotted Sandra with Ballybogy Snow Queen, who looked glorious. Lighting up one of the walking areas, her white fur dazzled, the lion clip contrasting the pom-pom coat with surprisingly muscular legs. She already had two challenge certificates and success would crown her as a champion and take her to Crufts.

Sandra was thrilled with Aed's progress. "He's looking great. You'd never know he'd been the runt. Eh boy. Good dog." She bent down to stroke his head, then stopped and squatted beside him.

"What on earth have you got on your ears?"

She looked at my dad.

He looked away and muttered, "Just a bit of plasticine. I wanted to be sure the cock was right."

Sandra burst out laughing. "I never heard the like. Plasticine. Wherever did you get the idea?"

He didn't answer.

"Is there a problem with his ears? Because if there is, a bit of plasticine won't make the slightest difference, once you've taken it off. And one thing's for sure, you can't leave it on."

"No, no. The ears are fine really. I just wanted to be sure." He laughed half-heartedly. "Anyway, we mustn't hold you back any longer."

I went with my dad to get the dogs kennelled. It was noisy in the queue, dogs barking and occasionally snapping at each other. My dad and I were silent, at least for the first few minutes. But suddenly he was shouting, "Ahh! Jesus Christ!"

He kicked out at a golden retriever. The dog growled, and its owner joined in with, "What do you think you're doing? How dare you kick my dog?"

"The bloody mangy thing's just pissed all over my leg."

I looked down. A wet stain ran from halfway down his calf. His desert boots were splashed with dog pee. It appeared the dog had mistaken my dad's leg for a tree and lifted his leg against it. I hid my delight behind a false cough.

"Jesus Christ," my dad said again. "Can't you keep that mongrel under control."

He went off to get cleaned up, leaving me in the queue with the dogs. He was gone ages, and there were only two people ahead of us by the time he returned. His trouser leg was sopping wet by now, and he seemed almost to be limping, dragging his leg slightly behind him.

The golden retriever owner had just finished registering, and my father gave a poisoned glare to his retreating back. It was our turn. He filled in the relevant paperwork, then we took the dogs off to their allocated stalls.

I removed the plasticine from Aed's ears and gave him a thorough grooming while my dad got Goldie settled. Then we left the dogs and joined the rest of the family for hotdogs from a food van.

Goldie's classes were first. He wasn't placed and my dad took him back to his stall. Soon it was Aed's turn. My dad reread his sheet of top ring tips, leaving me to groom him again. He looked fantastic. The judge thought so, too. He took first prize in Shetland sheepdog puppy and was runner-up in Shetland sheepdog overall.

My father was cock-a-hoop. "Oh, I knew you were a winner. I just knew it."

Sandra came over to congratulate him.

"He's got a big future," she said.

Little did she know how prophetic her words would be. In his next four shows, Aed was second, second, first and second. And then he stopped being placed. The first time my father put it down to the "imbecile judge", but on the third failure he demanded an explanation.

"Your dog is too tall."

Aed was far from the undersize specimen my dad had feared. My dad had given him so much Stress that he'd grown too big for the breed standard.

It looked like my dad's show days were over, till someone introduced him to Big Sammy, and obedience shows offered a lifeline. He was determined to give it his all. And a few holidaymakers on Portrush's family beach on bank holiday Monday weren't going to stand in his way.

Chapter 9

The Clipboard

ONE SATURDAY MORNING in May my sister's eleven-plus exam result arrived. Her whole future depended on what was written on that bit of paper. If she passed she'd go to Coleraine High, the Protestant girls' grammar. If she failed she'd be on her way to the scrapheap via Coleraine Girls' Secondary. My mother came into our bedroom to tell her the news.

"Has my result come through?" Joanna said.

"Yes, darling, it has. You're going to be going to the Secondary."

Joanna started to cry.

"I've failed. I've failed. I'm useless."

"There now, Joanna, don't be getting all het-up. It'll turn out fine in the end," my mother soothed, before leaving for work.

And maybe if my parents had been richer it would have turned out all right. If you failed the eleven-plus you could still get a grammar school education if your parents could afford to buy you one. Mary O'Brien from next door failed too, but her parents paid for her to go to the Catholic girls' grammar, Loreto Convent, instead of the Catholic secondary modern, Saint Joseph's.

My parents couldn't afford to pay for Joanna to go to the High, so in September she started at the Intermediate, as Coleraine Girls' Secondary was better known. The day she started, my father took a picture of her in her new, slightly too big, navy uniform. It was in the living room with the hideous patterned orange wallpaper as the backdrop. She looked pale and slight, tall but very thin, her long brown hair hanging down round her shoulders, fear leaping off her.

Her best friend from primary school, Jackie McLean, was going to the High, so Joanna was walking to her new school on her own. Her stammer was really bad then, especially when she got nervous. I looked at her and hoped she'd be OK.

I was starting primary five that day with a new teacher, Mrs MacElhinney. I loved school and was happy to be back. I missed it during the two-month summer holidays and would often cycle up there and ride around the grounds. I even found a small toilet window open one evening, slipping inside to wander the silent corridors to my primary four classroom. I sat at my desk for a while, back safe in my favourite place.

I had a great first day back—full marks in a snap spelling test and chocolate sponge with chocolate sauce for dessert at lunchtime. After school I went home, letting myself in with the back-door key, which still lived under the white paint pot in the garage. I cut myself a slice of the rhubarb tart my mother had made at the weekend, poured a glass of orange juice and took them through to the living room to enjoy over children's TV. Joanna arrived back about half an hour later, slumping into a chair and dropping her bag on the floor.

"So how'd it go?" I asked.

"Aye, not bad. Fine."

"What are your teachers like? I suppose you've got loads now you're at secondary school."

"I've only met the one so far, Miss Johnson, our form teacher. We stayed in our form room today. I'll start meeting the other teachers tomorrow when proper lessons get under way. I've got a timetable."

She produced a small lined book from her bag. A grid of days and times had been ruled on the back page.

"Tomorrow we start with double physics, with someone called Mr Walkingshaw in science lab 2. Then it's English in room 14 with Miss Johnson—she'll be teaching us English as well as being our form teacher. Then we've a break and then RE."

She went through the rest of her timetable with me.

"Oh, it's going to be great," I said to her. "All them subjects you're going to do. And the different teachers. And moving from one classroom to another. What do you think that'll be like? Will you not get lost?"

"Miss Johnson said that for the first few days at the end of each class the teacher will tell you where to go next. So I think I'll be OK."

For the first few weeks Joanna seemed to be settling in. She even made a new friend, Susan, who travelled in from Articlave on the bus. Towards the end of September, my father got elected as a parent-governor at her school. Well, I say elected; in fact he was the only candidate, though he kept that fact to himself. The first governors' meeting took place a few days later, on the last Friday afternoon of the month. At tea, the usual Friday-night fish and chips, he regaled us with details of his vital interventions.

"Well, as I said to Edith, you can't make an omelette without breaking eggs."

Edith was Miss Gilmer, the headmistress. He took to turning up early for governors' meetings, hoping for the opportunity to quiz her on some detail or other of the running of the school: the purchase of paper towels for the toilets or the lack of attention to Scottish history in my sister's education. He would pump my sister for information the week beforehand.

"How many teachers are there? Are there any vacancies? Are any teachers pregnant? How many toilets are blocked in a typical week? Is the third oven fixed in domestic science lab 1? Are the portions of chips big enough? How many girls are wearing non-regulation shoes or earrings?"

She'd answer as best as she could, and if she didn't know she'd have to try to get the information before the meeting. Everything she said was noted on his clipboard, which he'd take with him to the meetings.

As time went on, he'd pop in not only for the governors' meetings, but on other occasions too, always with his clipboard, recording anything and everything he could think of, from which of the fire doors squeaked, to which windows needed to be repainted, to the names of two girls he caught smoking down by the playing fields.

My sister dreaded bumping into him at school and would slink round the corridors, trying to look invisible, if she thought he might be around. On governors' days, she'd not even go to the canteen for lunch for fear of meeting him. Instead, she'd go straight to the safety of her form room at the far end of the school after morning lessons.

Even so, Joanna was enjoying school. She handed over her first report at breakfast on a Friday morning in December. My mother opened it. She threw her arms around my sister's neck. We weren't a very huggy family, so I knew it was something big. Tears were glistening in her eyes.

"Oh, Joanna," she said, "I'm so proud of you. You've done really well in your exams. They think you could get your review if you want to try for it. It would mean you'd be able to go to the High next September. You'd have to start again in the first year, but sure, wouldn't it be worth it?"

Joanna sat quietly for a while. "What will Daddy think about it?"

"What do you mean? He'll be thrilled, like I am. Why don't you run up and tell him. He's just finishing shaving."

"You go, Mummy," she said. "You tell him."

But neither of them had to move because at that moment he came clattering down the stairs, swearing under his breath.

"Bloody razor. Fucking useless."

The more little pieces of newspaper that were stuck to the flesh around his neck and face, the more you knew to steer clear of him. Shaving was not his favourite activity, and to judge from how often he applied the scraps of paper to stop the nicks bleeding, he wasn't very good at it. Today's half a dozen was not a good count.

My mother poured him a cup of tea and popped some bread under the grill for his toast while my father dragged a chair back from the table. He sat down, still muttering about the razor, touching his face gingerly now and again to check the sore spots. My mother brought the toast over to the table and then fetched the marmalade from the fridge.

"Any post yet?" he said.

"There's a brown one for you. I think it's the gas bill. I left it in the hall."

Why did she mention that? I thought. *Can she not see the mood he's in?*

"Oh, and Joanna's had her report from school," she added, almost as an afterthought. "They think she should go for her review."

He finished his mouthful of toast and took a gulp of his tea before speaking.

"Well done," he said eventually. "You must be pleased." He looked straight at Joanna.

She dropped her eyes and nodded.

"Isn't it great she might get to the High? She'll get a proper education," my mum said.

"A proper education!" he exploded. "I'd've thought at least in my own home there'd be recognition of everything me and the other governors are doing to make education at the Secondary every bit as good as at the High."

"Now, Victor, you know I didn't mean it like that. I just want Joanna to get the best chance."

"And you're saying that I don't? I'm only thinking of Joanna. Maybe you're the one with ulterior motives. You've never got over not getting to grammar school. Now you're wanting to move her about like a sack of potatoes, when she's just got settled, when she's doing so well."

My mother opened her mouth to say something but he cut her short. "I'm away to my work," he said, and went out slamming the door.

"I'm s-sorry," Joanna said. "If I hadn't done s-so well, then there wouldn't be a p-problem."

Little was spoken over tea that night and nothing on the subject of my sister's future education. Afterwards my dad went upstairs to get changed. He was bowling that night, in with a chance to win a turkey. I got on with feeding the dogs, dividing a large tin of Chump between their bowls before adding a generous sprinkling of Winalot and a little warm water. I left them eating in the garden. He was running down the stairs as I came back into the house.

"I'm off," he said. "Tell your mother I might be late."

I helped Joanna with the dishes, then we joined my mum in the living room. She was humming to herself and didn't look up. I asked her what she wanted to watch, but she didn't answer, just carried on humming. I went over to her.

"Are you all right?" I said.

"What?" she said, coming to. "Yes, yes, I'm fine. Everything's fine."

She looked over at the TV. "Away and bring me the paper and we'll see what's on the telly."

Joanna went back to school after Christmas. By the time her next report arrived, her results had dropped off. Although she wasn't at the bottom of the class, she slipped back towards the middle in everything but art. With the review problem out of the way, my father threw himself into his work as a school governor. He upped his activity, volunteering for the interview panel on every vacancy that arose. When he saw the successful candidates, he'd remind them of his role in their appointment.

Parents' evenings were a particular trial for Joanna. My mother spent the evening trying to find out how Joanna was doing, my father letting the staff and other parents know that he was a governor. Her third year parents' evening was aimed at helping decide what subjects she should take for CSE. My sister wasn't sure what she should choose. The only thing she knew for certain was that she wanted to do art.

The parents' evening was due to start at 6.30 p.m. As so often, my mother was running late. My parents had arrived home by car at a quarter to six and we'd had our tea immediately. It was my favourite—sausage, bean and potato pie— and I'd put it in the oven in plenty of time and was serving it on to plates as they walked through the door.

As soon as he'd eaten, my father went upstairs to change into his standard smart-casual: brown slacks, beige shirt, brown striped tie and brown checked sports coat. He even had time to run his electric shaver (Simon, Joanna and I had clubbed together for one the previous Christmas) over the day's growth.

At six-fifteen he was sitting in his chair in the living room, clipboard on knee, drawing up a schedule of teachers to see, issues to cover. My sister sat silently on the sofa, her opinion neither sought nor offered.

Meanwhile, my mother was still thudding about upstairs, searching for a dress that looked respectable, tights that weren't laddered and lipstick that matched her outfit.

"Maisie, what's keeping you?" he shouted up the stairs at twenty past six.

He came back into the living room.

"Away up and see what your bloody mother's up to," he said to me.

I found her in the bedroom panicking about where she'd put her purse.

"Sure you're not going to need any money, are you?" I said.

"Oh, no, I suppose not. Stupid," she said.

She ran her hands over her pale green dress and looked in the mirror.

"Do I look all right?" she said.

"Aye. You look great," I answered. "You best go down, they're waiting for you."

"Jesus, Maisie, will you come on," we heard my father shout. "I've got my position to consider."

"See you later," she said to me and went to join them.

I did my homework in front of the telly with the dogs at my feet. Upstairs, music pounded out from our Simon's room where he, too, was working. It was just after nine when the car pulled up outside the house. My mother and sister got out; my dad reversed and drove away.

"Where's Daddy going?" I asked.

"He's away to see someone about paving slabs or something," my mother answered. "Away and put on the kettle, would you, Constance, for a cup of tea."

My sister joined me in the kitchen.

"So, how was it?" I asked.

She rolled her eyes, then laughed.

"Oh, you know what he's like when he gets going with the clipboard. Asking questions about all sorts. I was expecting him to find out what they'd had for lunch next. He kept holding his left hand up, stopping them so he could write up his notes on the clipboard." She laughed again. "Honest to God, I could've died. We took ages with every teacher. Far longer than anyone else. He nearly got into a fight with Carol Campbell's dad over it."

"What happened?"

"Well, you know how he is about Scottish history. He'd been talking on to Miss McMorris about it when Mr Campbell said to him, 'Will you stop ganshing on. There's other people here waiting to speak to the teachers.'"

"No! So what did my da do?"

"He said, 'Sir, I am Governor McCullagh, here to sort out my daughter's future. Please have some patience.' "

"I thought Mr Campbell would hit him there and then, but instead he said, 'I don't care if you're Jesus Christ himself. You're not keeping me and our Carol waiting half the night. You and your bloody clipboard.' "

"Miss McMorris had to step in. She told my da to call her if there was anything else and then got on with Mr Campbell instead."

"Oh," I said. "She's one of the ones you like, isn't she?"

"Aye, she's wile nice. My da liked her, too. Until tonight. Now he's saying he always knew there was something fishy about her. I hope he doesn't get her into big trouble."

She sat silent for a minute.

"So what subjects do you think you're going to do?" I asked. "Are you any the wiser?"

"Well, not history. He says I'm not doing it while Miss McMorris is the teacher, even though it's one of my best subjects. And we didn't get round all the other teachers because he took so long. But I'm definitely doing both English language and literature and biology, which I hate. He said it was a good one to have in your locker. Said I could go on to be a dental nurse or a vet's assistant. Can you imagine?"

I'd always wanted to be a vet, right up until the previous summer, when my dad had Goldie put down. Said it was because his bad hip was giving him too much pain, though maybe it wouldn't have if my dad hadn't kept kicking him in the leg. Whatever, he was put down, and two weeks later my dad arrived home with a six-month-old Alsatian that he'd bought from Big Sammy.

"So what do you want to do?" I asked Joanna.

She shrugged. "Who knows? But he's putting me down for French—says it's good to have a language. Typing. Maths. And domestic science."

"Domestic science? Sure he hates what you bring home from cookery classes."

"I know, but he says I need to master it."

"So what about art? I thought that was the only one you were certain about?"

"He says it's a waste of time. If I want to draw, sure I can do it in my spare time. Maybe he's right."

"What did your art teacher say?"

"We didn't get to see her."

"What about Mummy?"

"What about me?" my mother said behind me.

"Oh nothing. Just about whether Joanna can do art. It's her favourite subject, but Daddy doesn't want her to do it."

She sat down at the table. "I'll talk to him about the art. OK? Now where's that cup of tea you were making fifteen minutes ago? I think I fancy some toast as well. Does anyone else want some?"

There was a week between the parents' evening and the date set for finalising her choices. On the eve of the deadline, Joanna asked my dad to complete the form authorising the choices. He sent her off to get his clipboard from the box where he stored all of the information about the school.

"Now what had we decided?" he said. "Oh yes. English language, English literature, French, maths, biology, domestic science and typing."

My sister's eyes flicked sideways to my mother. A silent plea crossed the table. My mother looked down for a moment, then raising her head she said, "Oh, Victor. What about Joanna maybe doing art? Perhaps instead of the domestic science? Sure she enjoys it."

There was a pause while my father put the top back on his pen. Finally he looked up.

"I have investigated that option, but I'm afraid it just doesn't work timetable wise. She'd have to give up typing as well as domestic science. And clearly that's not in her best interests. So I think we should stick with my original plan, don't you?"

My mother sighed but didn't say anything.

"Is there n-no other w-way I could f-fit it in, Daddy?" Joanna said.

"No, there's not."

The discussion was over. He signed the bottom of the form and handed it back to Joanna.

"Thanks," she said, taking it from him.

Chapter 10

Christian Endeavour

IN 1974 I joined Christian Endeavour, which met every Thursday afternoon at the First Coleraine church hall. Mrs Fitzsimons, the driving force behind Christain Endeavour in Coleraine, was deeply impressed by my Bible knowledge. I'd win a Marathon most weeks in the quiz. I loved it. And in 1976 Mrs Fitzsimons persuaded me that a Christian Endeavour holiday in Donaghadee would be even more fun.

I wasn't keen at first. I'd been on a Good News Club holiday the year before: a whole week sleeping in a camp-bed in a school outside Castlerock, praying and reading the Bible for hours on end, with no TV and no radio, and mainly Plymouth Brethren children for light entertainment. But Mrs Fitzsimons was a persistent woman.

"Sure, Constance, you'll love it," she told me in her lilting Dublin voice. "You'll absolutely love it. It's a proper Christian holiday centre, now, the place in Donaghadee. Not some nasty draughty old school. It has proper dormitories with bunk-beds and a TV room and everything. And the Ards Peninsula? Sure it's a great place to be exploring."

It was the dormitories that sealed it. I loved Enid Blyton, and this was as near as I would come to the midnight feasts and practical jokes of Malory Towers.

My dad dropped me off at the gate just after lunch on the Saturday afternoon.

"You'll be all right from here," he said.

It was a lonely walk up towards the big house with my duffle bag, suitcase and letter, advising me to report to Miss Richards on arrival. I didn't know Miss Richards or anyone else. The house was an old, solid, converted vicarage. At least it looked friendly. As I walked up the drive, I spotted a girl doing perfect handstands on the lawn. She started to walk forward on her hands, legs hanging in the air above her. I couldn't help but say, "You're good," as I passed her.

Instantly she was upright, grinning at me. It was quite a smile.

"Thanks," she said. "I'm Maggie. Who are you?"

"Constance," I answered.

"Are you here for the Christian Endeavour week?"

I nodded.

"Me, too," she said.

"I've got to check in with someone called Miss Richards. Do you know where I'd find her?"

"Oh, Heather," she said, smiling again. "She's really nice. If you've been given her name, you're probably in the same dorm as me. Come on, I'll show you."

I followed her up the stone steps and into the house. The hallway was tiled in black and cream, laid out in a checked pattern. A wide staircase ahead branched to both left and right. We took the left-hand flight and proceeded to a large room at the back of the house. It contained three sets of wooden bunk-beds and half a dozen lockers. A young woman was unpacking at one of them. She was one of the most beautiful women I'd ever seen—tall and slim with shiny black hair, dancing green eyes and full red lips.

"That's her," Maggie said to me.

The young woman smiled at me and I felt myself redden.

"Were you looking for me?" she said.

I nodded, blushing even deeper.

"What's your name?"

"Constance," I said.

She took a list from the back pocket of her jeans. "Constance McCullagh, is it?"

I nodded.

"You're in my group. This is your dorm. Choose yourself a bed. Maggie there's already bagsed the top one by the window and I'm here near the door, but the rest are free."

I stood, hesitating, not knowing which one to choose. Maggie solved the problem.

"Take the one below me," she said.

So I did. I took my pyjamas out of my duffle bag and laid them on the bed. I looked out the window. There was another lawn on this side of the house, but this one had a badminton net stretched across it. And beyond it was an orchard. I liked it here.

"Have you brought your plates with you?" Heather asked.

"Yes," I said.

We'd been instructed to bring an unbreakable plate, bowl and cup. My granda had bought me a white enamel set, edged in dark blue. I got them out to show her.

"You'll need to take them down to the kitchen. Maggie'll show you where. Then you're free until four when we're all meeting up in the main hall downstairs. OK?"

I spent the afternoon with Maggie, climbing trees in the orchard, cartwheeling round the lawn. As the afternoon wore on, more children joined us, in ones and twos, and then a group of four who arrived together. Maggie knew quite a few of them. Like her, they were mostly from Belfast.

Just before four, Heather came out and called us in. We filed into the hall, those who knew each other pushing and shoving in a good-natured way.

"Settle down now," a white-haired woman called out. Her voice was sharp and southern. I wondered if she knew Mrs Fitzsimons.

"That's better," she said. "Now, I'd like to welcome you to this Christian Endeavour week." She bowed her head suddenly.

"Dear Father in heaven, bless all the children who have come here to learn more about your everlasting love. Bless the teachers and leaders who offer up their service to you this week. Through them please guide these children that they might follow your path. Amen."

Around the room, children echoed, "Amen."

Having got the praying out of the way, she proceeded to the rules for the week:

"You will do what the teachers and leaders tell you.
"There will be no running inside the house.
"There will be no shouting inside the house.
"There will be no swearing.
"And every team will contribute to the chores around the house this week, as directed by your dorm leader."

She paused for a moment. "I hope that is all clear, and woe betide you if I catch any of you with so much as a toe out of line. Now I'll hand you over to Miss Richards for the quiz."

The quiz consisted of alternating rounds of Biblical and

general knowledge, with teams based on dorms. There were three other girls in our team—Lindsay and Ruth, who Maggie knew from Belfast, and Karen from Portadown. Between us our general knowledge wasn't bad, but it was my Bible knowledge that really gave our team the edge.

"You're really good at this," Maggie said, as we surged ahead. "How come you know all this?"

I just smiled and winked at her.

After the quiz we had tea and then telly. Mrs Fitzsimons was right—this camp was going to be fun. But I got nervous when it was time to go to bed. I didn't want to get changed in front of the others and took my pyjamas through to the toilets. I felt better once I was ready for bed and padded back to the dorm in my slippers. I was just about to get into my bunk when out of the corner of my eye I noticed something moving. Then I shuddered. It was an earwig.

I was terrified of earwigs. When I was little, Joanna kept telling me that an earwig would sneak into my ear when I was asleep, then crawl into my brain and send me mad. At home I slept with cotton wool in my ears. My mum had put some tissues in my duffle bag. They were in my locker. I kept my eye on the earwig for as long as I could, but to open my locker I had to turn my back on it. I opened my cupboard and found the tissues, but I couldn't get the box open, fighting with the perforations. At last I freed a couple of tissues. As I wadded them, ready for squashing the earwig, I heard Maggie exclaim, "Good shot!" I turned back towards the wall. "Hey, Constance," she said to me, "Lindsay just flicked some insect six feet across the room."

Some insect? Oh God, please not the earwig.

"Was it an earwig?" I asked.

"An earwig?" she said.

"Yes, an earwig. Was it an earwig?"

"Yes, I think it was. Those are the black skinny ones, aren't they?"

I started to panic.

"Where did it land?" I said.

"What?"

"Where did it land? Did either of you see it land? Was it still alive?"

I started scouring the floor. Where was it? Where had it gone?

"Are you OK, Constance?" Maggie asked. She sounded nervous. "It was just an earwig."

I forced out a laugh. I didn't want to tell her how worried I was that the earwig would send me mad. I knew I was too old still to believe my sister's stories. I couldn't explain, even to myself, why the fear still had me in its grip.

"Yes. Sorry. Yes, I'm fine," I said. I laughed again, though it sounded false in my ears. "I just don't like earwigs very much."

Maggie laughed too, but I could see she was still wary. "No, they're ugly. Wee hooky arses on them. Still they're harmless enough, aren't they? It's wasps I can't stand. I got stung on the lip when I was four. It blew up like a balloon. Nasty, buzzy, stinging wee gets."

Miss Richards returned from the bathroom. "Hurry up, you two, and get into bed. It's lights out in two minutes." Maggie hauled herself up to the top bunk. I glanced round my bed, checking as best as I could that the earwig wasn't there. I got into bed. A minute later the lights were out.

There was some sniggering and whispering for a few

minutes, but soon everyone settled down. I heard Maggie above me move over into sleep. But I lay stiff with terror, fingers stuffed in my ears. I couldn't sleep, kept crushing imaginary earwigs against my face to stop them getting to my ears. And when I finally did drop off, I dreamt about an earwig.

I was back at home, lying in my bed asleep. And at the same time I was watching me lying in my bed at home asleep. I spotted a small earwig near the bedroom door. It started to creep towards me. As it got closer, it got bigger, and bigger. Then it reared up on its back two legs. It was six feet tall now, towering over me. But still I lay sleeping. I needed to wake, try to escape, but I couldn't. I couldn't. And then it was too late. The earwig was on top of me. It was crushing me, grinding me into the bed. I couldn't breathe, couldn't breathe. I needed to scream, but it wouldn't come out. And then I started to scream, screaming in my dream.

Suddenly I woke up. I was sitting up in bed. My heart was thumping. The room was dark—pitch black. Thick, black night. I was frightened. The scream was there in my throat, but I didn't think it had come out. Around me everyone seemed still to be asleep.

I'd had this dream before, at home. I'd usually slip into bed behind Joanna after it, but I couldn't do that tonight. I tried to take deep breaths, but I was gulping. I peered all around, looking for the giant earwig. It wasn't there. I needed to calm down. In my head, I started singing about my favourite things, like Julie Andrews advised. But they kept mutating into something horrible—kittens with their tongues cut out, mittens filled with writhing worms. I could feel the sick fear in the back of my throat. I started to rock, back and forth, back and forth.

And then I felt a hand on my arm. I started.

"Constance. Are you OK? It's me. Heather. Miss Richards."

I started to sob. She put her arms around me.

"Shhh!" she said. "It's all right. Don't worry. You're OK. It's only a week. You'll be home again on Saturday. And we'll have such fun this week. Honestly, I promise."

She stroked my hair. It calmed me. I started to drift into a safer sleep.

I woke to a grey day, light drizzle speckling the window. I looked around. A couple of the other girls were stirring too, and Heather's bed was already empty. She appeared at the doorway, wearing a smart blue dress.

"Rise and shine, sleepyheads," she said. "It's breakfast in fifteen minutes."

I got up first and made my way to the bathroom. As I passed, Heather said quietly, "Are you OK?" She put her hand on my arm. I blushed.

"Yes, thanks," I mumbled.

I washed and dressed quickly, ready for church later that morning. But first we had breakfast, Bible reading and chores. Our dorm helped prepare the Sunday lunch, peeling potatoes and scrubbing carrots. After lunch a woman who used to be a missionary came to tell us all about her work in Africa. We were all gripped by her story of a young boy torn between Jesus and obeying his parents.

I was nervous again going to bed that night. But Heather came up to me and said, "If you get upset or frightened in the night, just come and wake me up. OK? I won't mind. Not in the least. Promise me you'll wake me if you need me."

I nodded. "I promise. Thank you." My head had barely

touched the pillow that night before I was asleep, and I made it through till morning without waking.

Monday whizzed past with breakfast, chores, Bible study, a treasure hunt, lunch, discussion group, the beach, tea and telly. Tuesday and Wednesday followed a similar pattern. Thursday was the best day yet, with rounders in the morning and crazy golf in the afternoon. Heather led the discussion in the afternoon on the importance of love in Christian teaching.

"Don't Go Breaking My Heart" was still number one on *Top of the Pops* that evening. While we were getting ready for bed, Maggie and I did an impression of Elton John and Kiki Dee to the amusement of the rest of the dorm.

Friday was a bright and sunny day. We were going on a boat trip to the Copeland Islands' bird sanctuary, but we had an hour free after Bible study. Maggie and I decided to play badminton on the back lawn. There were about nine or ten of us, crowded on both sides of the net. There wasn't much space to play, but we were all having a good time, pushing and shoving each other to get to the shuttle. And in one of those battles, I got whacked in the face by a badminton racket. It caught me just above the right eye, broke the racket. I could feel the lump rising.

"Are you all right?" It was Maggie. "Come and sit down." She led me to the side.

"I'm fine, really," I said.

"Heather will be here in a minute. Lindsay went to fetch her."

"There was no need. Really, I'm fine."

I stood up. I felt a bit woozy but I carried on. "I'll just go and splash a bit of water on it. I'll be right as rain."

I ran into Heather at the door to the house.

"Are you OK?"

"Yeah, it's just a bit of a lump. I'll be fine."

"Maybe you should go and lie down, take it easy for the rest of the day."

"No way," I said. "I want to come on the boat trip. It's the last day."

"OK, OK. But don't overdo it."

I loved being out on the water. It wasn't a large boat, but it was sturdy, slapping along over the waves. I sat next to Maggie. She was a beige-green colour.

"Oh, I don't like boats," she moaned. "Get me off here."

We got off at the largest of the three Copeland Islands. There was a small beach.

"Oh, look at all these tiny shells," Heather said. Strewn across the beach, in piles near the rocks, were tiny snail-shaped shells. "They're so beautiful."

I quickly gathered some shells and stuffed them in my pockets to give to Heather later. My chance came that evening, just before tea. I'd wrapped them up as best as I could in a tissue.

"Oh, these are lovely," she said. "Thank you so much."

"I'll miss you."

"I'll miss you, too, Constance. Have you had a good time?"

I nodded. "It's gone quickly." Too quickly. I wasn't ready to go home yet. I wished I could stay for another week.

"Constance, is everything all right?"

"What do you mean?"

"I don't know. I'm just worried about you. Sometimes you seem so tough. Like this morning, someone breaks a racket over your head and there's not even a tear. But others, like now, it seems like the slightest touch might break you."

She put her arm out towards me, but I flinched away, tears starting in my eyes.

"Constance, what's wrong? I can see that something is. What is it?"

"Nothing," I said, but the tears were spilling now.

"That's not true," she said. "Something's troubling you. I can see it. You can tell me. It'll be OK."

Part of me wanted to. But then she'd know what I was really like. And it wouldn't be OK. So I swallowed hard, brushed away the tears.

"I'll just miss you. That's all."

Chapter 11

Clumpy Shoes

MY PRIMARY SCHOOL was sponsored by the Honourable the Irish Society. Based in the City of London, it had been given a great chunk of Ireland, including Coleraine, by James II in the seventeenth century.

The school's heavy wrought-iron gates bearing the school's crest—the Red Hand of Ulster, topped by a crown, flanked by two fern leaves along with the motto "God Direct Us"—had been paid for by the Irish Society. But perhaps the most obvious sign of its link to the school was the annual prize-giving ceremony in June.

Preparations began weeks beforehand. All prizewinners would be hauled out of class to practise for the ceremony for hours at a time. The practices were overseen by our fearsome spinster head, Miss Millington. A tall, stern woman, she didn't let her dislike of small children stand in the way of running a primary school.

My first practice was in June 1973. The hall was empty, save for Miss Millington and Mrs Cooke from the office, when I arrived with the other winners from my class. We'd been summoned by a messenger from Miss Millington.

"What class are you?" she barked at Tracy Barr.

"Primary 3a, Miss Millington."

"Excellent. Right, academic prizewinners, I want you to line up here in the front row in the order in which you were placed. Arts and crafts winners can go and sit at the back for now." I'd won both an academic and a crafts prize but was too frightened of Miss Millington to mention it. I shuffled into position with the other academic winners.

"Come along, come along," Miss Millington said. "I've not got all day. I've got other classes arriving." She turned to 3b who were hovering by the door. "I'll be with you in a minute. In the meantime, please be quiet." Then back to us. "Right, you can sit down now. These are your starting places. Memorise them."

She filled in 3b behind us, then 4a and 4b and up through the school as far as 6b. By now the primary 7s had arrived.

"Can the Top Six come forward please. Children, this is Jenny, Roger, Mark, Karen, Amy and George. They are the Top Six pupils in this school. The best of the best. These are the children to look up to, to aspire to. This school is proud of them. Their parents are proud of them. And maybe if you work hard, you can make it into the Top Six in your final year and make us all proud of you, too."

The Top Six took their places, followed by the rest of the primary 7 winners.

"Right, that was the easy part. Now it's time to put the arts and crafts prizewinners in order. How many of you academic prizewinners have also won a craft prize?"

I put my hand up. There was one other in primary 3, a boy from 3b, and a similar smattering throughout the year groups. There were three prizes for each year group for girls' crafts and three for boys'. Miss Millington started to put them in order, leaving gaps for any academic winners who'd also won a prize. The bell for break time rang.

"There's not time for break today," Miss Millington said. "We've got far too much to do."

There were a few whisperings among the children.

"Silence," Miss Millington said. "We are here to prepare for the most important event of the school year. Your break time is a small sacrifice."

At last everyone was in place.

"All right, children. May I have your complete attention," Miss Millington said. "This school is privileged to be associated with the Honourable the Irish Society. It is down to each of you to uphold our position. The Irish Society gives up its hard-earned money to give all of you a better education. It is the least that you can do that you show your immense gratitude to them for their unflagging generosity. Our guests are very important men from the City of London, and they're coming here especially to see you. I want you all to think about what an honour that is. You will show them all the respect that they deserve.

"Now, what do I mean by respect? I mean clean hair, clean faces, clean uniforms. I mean dry cool hands, not filthy sweaty mitts. I mean saying "thank you" loud and clear. I mean curtsying for girls and bowing for boys. I mean not speaking unless you're spoken to, and I mean singing out your gratitude strong and true when it comes to the national anthem at the end. Do you understand me?"

I wasn't 100 per cent sure that I followed everything she'd said, but I answered, "Yes, Miss Millington," with the other children.

"All right then. Down to business."

We started with Miss Millington leaving the assembly hall and then returning as if she were showing the Honourable the Irish Society to their seats on the platform. "As soon as I walk into this hall," she shouted over her shoulder, as she continued to mime her way on to the stage, muttering and gesticulating to her imaginary guests, "you will all stand. You will remain standing until the entire party is seated. I will then give you the following signal." She turned around and gave a discreet palm-down gesture with her right hand. "You will then be seated. All right, let's run that through."

She left the hall again, then re-entered with the party of the Honourable the Irish Society. We leapt to our feet, accompanied by the scraping and banging of 100 wooden chairs on the hall's wooden floor. She turned upon us.

"What was all of that dreadful din? That was completely unacceptable. Are you animals? You must stand up quickly but QUIETLY."

Miss Millington then demonstrated with one of the platform chairs how it should be done. "Sit towards the edge of the seat. Then place your feet on the floor about shoulder width apart. Rise from your seat in one movement, rooting your feet into the floor. Root and rise," she said, lifting noiselessly from her chair. "That's the secret." She sat back down again. And then stood one more time. "Root and rise, root and rise."

We practised a few times, and although it was an improvement, Miss Millington was far from satisfied. "Don't move your feet. The next child that I see move his or her feet will get three from Wilbur."

Wilbur was her cane, which she used to lash the bare hands of unfortunate pupils. Certainly no one could accuse

Miss Millington of spoiling the child. She rarely went any-where without Wilbur. Today he sat ominously on one of the chairs on the stage.

We practised again. There was a large clatter. I turned towards its source. A large, lumpy-looking boy in primary 6 seemed to have knocked the chair in front. Maybe he'd had an over-enthusiastic rise without enough of a root.

"Peter McAllister. Get up here now, you horrible boy."

The clumsy boy made his way to the front.

"Come on, right up here, right on to the stage."

He climbed the five wooden steps and walked across the stage to stand in front of her.

"There's only one way to make you learn. Hand out."

He held out his right hand, palm upward. She laid the last few inches of her cane along it, getting her line. Then slowly she lifted her arm, pausing, before bringing it down swiftly across his bare hand. Those of us near the front heard the cane swish through the air before it slapped down on its target.

There was a slight flicker in Peter's eyes as each stroke landed. But otherwise his expression didn't change.

"Now back to your place. And if there's any more non-sense, it'll be the end of prize-giving for you.

"Let's try once more. Root and rise. Root and rise."

You could almost hear the concentration, one hundred minds focused on the same silent task. This time no one had a mishap.

"Getting better," she said. "Now let's try it from the top."

She left the hall for a third time and then returned with the same platform-party pantomime. We rose as one with only the slightest murmur of chairs. Miss Millington carried on up the steps and showed her imaginary guests to their seats. She turned, gave us the signal and we sat quietly back down.

"Excellent! Excellent, children! I knew you could do it. Now, let's prepare for the next part. On the day I will give a few introductory words, and then the governor of the Honourable the Irish Society will present the prizes. Today Mrs Cooke will be acting in his stead."

When she returned, Miss Millington took up position at the far left-hand side of the stage. She held a hard-backed book. Mrs Cooke joined her a few feet further in.

"Before we start, let me explain how the prize-giving will operate," Miss Millington said. "I will call out a category. For example class prizes, primary 3a."

I listened hard. Primary 3a was my class.

"That category will move from their seats in line, to take up position from the top of the right-hand steps. I will then call out each child's name. You will walk quickly across the stage to Mrs Cooke. If you are a boy, you will give a short bow." She demonstrated. "Girls will curtsy.

"Mrs Cooke will give you your prize. You will take it with your left hand. You will say 'thank you', loudly and clearly, while you offer your right hand. Mrs Cooke will take your hand and shake it. You will then leave the stage. If you are a craft winner, you will take your place among the other craft winners. The rest of you will take seats in the empty rows immediately behind the prizewinners. Is that all clear?"

I felt a surge of panic. There was so much to remember. But I said, "Yes, Miss Millington," along with everyone else.

"Let's start the prize-giving. Class prizes. Primary 3a."

The ten of us got up from our seats and took up our

prize-receiving positions. I was eighth. Tracy Barr had been first. She waited nervously at the top of the steps for Miss Millington to call out her name. But first there were yet more instructions.

"Primary 3b, can you move to line up behind 3a? And the rest of you move forward a row so that 4a are where 3a have just been, 4b where 3b were. That way the next group of prizewinners is always at the front."

At last Miss Millington started calling out the names of the prizewinners. I felt a prickle of excitement as my name was called. I made it across the stage without tripping, performed an acceptable curtsy and got my hands in the right order for the handshake and book.

I left the stage and found my seat amongst the arts and crafts prizewinners. I'd won the primary 3 girls' prize with my embroidered table mat. William Murray, second with his papier mâché Donald Duck, took the other vacant seat in primary 3 crafts. The rest of primary 3 filled up the newly empty seats at the back of the prizewinners.

Miss Millington proceeded with the primary 4, 5 and 6 prizewinners, the Top Six and the rest of primary 7. The arts and crafts prizes followed, and finally the sports cups. The run-through had taken two hours without a break. We finished with a prayer of thanks and were halfway through the national anthem when the dinner bell rang.

"Well, children," she said. "I'm pleased we're making progress, but we need to speed up. The Irish Society won't have all day, you know. You can go and have lunch now, but there's no time for play. I want you all back in your seats in half an hour's time. We start again at five past one."

We got the rehearsal done in an hour and a half that

afternoon, and after three more practices that week, we were beating the hour.

Having sorted out the prizewinners, Miss Millington turned her attention to the rest of the school. They were lined up on either side of the long curving path that led from the school gates down to the main entrance and taught how to clap and give a loud and lively "hurray" in response to Miss Millington's "Three cheers for the Honourable the Irish Society. Hip Hip."

The school looked fantastic on prize-giving day. Two huge, lush ferns stood, one on either side of the main entrance. Inside, the school was festooned with flowers that had been sent in by parents and arranged by the Parent-Teachers Association the evening before. Gladioli, lupins and delphiniums stood tall in long glass vases. Creamy lilies scented the air. Tiny posies of pansies and violas had been scattered in between, and everywhere were bowls and vases of roses, of every possible shade and hue, some in full blossom, others still tight little buds.

At 10.15 the prizewinners were dispatched to the assembly hall. By 10.30 we were all seated, row upon row of clean, uniformed children. The governors started filling up the seats behind us, followed by some of the teachers.

I gazed up at the stage. There was a lectern at the left-hand side; a table nearby was covered with piles and piles of books. A dozen chairs sat towards the back of the platform, and a low table in front was adorned with a crystal bowl filled with blood-red roses.

I was ready for the ceremony to start, but the members of the Honourable the Irish Society weren't due until eleven. I kept looking at my watch and fidgeting in my seat. After what felt like five hours, we heard clapping and cheering. And then, "Hurray! . . . Hurray! . . . Hurray!"

After the long, slow build-up, time started sprinting now. One minute Miss Millington, magnificently severe in a midnight blue dress and fur-edged black gown, was showing the Irish Society party to their seats, the next I'd already collected my class prize and was on the steps for embroidery. At my second appearance on stage, the governor of the Irish Society, an immensely tall man in a long red robe and hefty gold chain, said to me, "I think you've been up before, haven't you?" His blue eyes sparkled under heavy grey brows.

"Yes, sir," I said, reddening.

"Jolly well done," he said. "Keep up the good work."

Over the following summer, I became obsessed with doing well at school. It was the turning-point summer after the Coleraine bombing. I was determined to come first. In the next year, as the exams approached, I started cramming my brain with spellings and sums and nature facts. The tests started on a Thursday in June with maths and spelling, then nature study on Friday, and reading and writing on Monday. The first couple of days went well, but over the weekend disaster struck. I thrust my hand into my pencil case on the Friday evening searching for my red felt tip and got a pencil lead embedded under the nail of my right index finger. When I woke the next morning, it was throbbing. I went to show my mum, finger held out before me.

"Will it be all right, Mummy? I've got my writing test on Monday?"

"I think it'll be fine. It's just a bit infected," she said. "A bread poultice should draw out the poison."

But it was still hurting on Monday morning. She took me

to the health centre when it opened at 8.30. The nurse applied disinfectant, a finger sock and a sling. I arrived at school just in time to take the test, but it was difficult to hold the pen firmly. I got only 6 out of 10. But I did so well on the other tests that it didn't matter—I was first by one mark over Mark Morrell.

There'd not been many books left to choose from when I'd been eighth in primary 3. I'd gone in the end for *Tinker the Kitten* because I loved animals. It was special to me because it was my first-ever book prize, and it had a label in the front with the school crest and my name on it. But it would never have been my first choice—too many pictures, not enough words. Primary 4 was different. I got first crack and I went for *Heidi*. I won again the next year and got *What Katy Did Next* and the year after *Little Women*.

Primary 7 was the big year though. The chance to be in the Top Six. I wanted it so badly. If I made it, my parents would be invited as guests to the prize-giving and to the buffet meal to follow with the Irish Society. And I'd get my photo in the local paper—officially I would be worth something.

I worked hard all year and began intensive preparation in the month before the exams. We'd been studying Mary Queen of Scots in history, and I committed every fact I could find about her to my memory: date of birth, year of engagement to the Dauphin, year of his death, second husband, alleged adultery, years and places of imprisonment, plots against Elizabeth, date of execution. I had it all there, ready to be summoned in an instant. It was the same with the other subjects. And the more I crammed, the more space I seemed to create in my mind for even more facts.

The rest of my class had no chance. I was top of my year by five clear marks. There were special subject prizes too in primary 7 and I won English and geography. I lost the religious education prize on a technicality: my marks were the best, but our class teacher, Mrs Lawson, awarded it to Clare for general Christian attitude. I was glad that at least it was going to my best friend. I won the knitting prize, too, and the sports cup.

Clare had been helping me win the sports cup for my year since it was introduced in 1974. She practised the two sports events where I needed a partner—the wheelbarrow and three-legged races—until we ran as one.

The prize-giving was held on a Tuesday. I woke to a beautiful day, sunny and warm. I had such high hopes as I arrived at school that morning. Today was the day that my dad would see for himself how good I was.

I wore my school uniform—grey pinafore, white shirt and red tie—but I wasn't wearing my normal school shoes. They had started hurting the week before, so instead I was wearing black wedges my mum had bought as a stopgap from the thrift shop where she took our old clothes. I resisted them that morning, wanted to wear my old ones. Although the wedges looked good with jeans, they were a bit clumpy for my school uniform. But my mum didn't want me hurting my feet:

"Sure it doesn't matter what they look like. You're only wearing them to and from school. You'll be changing into your plimsolls when you get there."

The school looked fantastic, as always on prize day. It was Silver Jubilee year, and a red, white and blue theme dominated the decorations. I paused to look at the flowers and then made my way down to the cloakroom where I changed my shoes.

Our class was already demob happy. We were only a few days from the end of primary school, and with our eleven-plus and exams well and truly over, Mrs Lawson had agreed we could do fun things like quizzes, crosswords and writing limericks. I think she regretted the last of these, when Jack Kennedy dared me to make up one about her:

> There once was a teacher called Lawson
> She hated that comic Les Dawson
> She liked a good sum
> And she had a big bum
> That teacher the preacher called Lawson

She was a good teacher, but her classes were dominated by two passions—maths and religion. She was a Free Presbyterian, Ian Paisley's church, and would talk at length about the teachings of the Bible. Unlike our previous teachers, she wouldn't permit us to draw Jesus or God in our RE workbooks. The only exception was for our lesson on the Sermon on the Mount, where we could include Jesus as long as it was from the back.

"It is blasphemy to draw the Lord's face," she said. "Who are we, mere broken sinners, to think we can imagine His face? The time for seeing His face is not now. No! That time will come only on Judgement Day when those of us who have accepted the Lord as our saviour, and walked in His light, will be called home. Only then, only then will we see His face."

Blasphemy was a big issue for Mrs Lawson. Horoscopes, lucky shamrocks, not walking under a ladder—all were blasphemy. Any form of work, including everything from heating up food to watching TV, was completely unacceptable on a Sunday. The Lord's day was for church and prayer only.

One of her favourite stories was about how God rewards those who keep His laws related to this strict Sunday observance. Her twin daughters were appearing in *Songs of Praise*, which had been recorded mid-week. But there was no way Mrs Lawson was going to be watching the broadcast, daughters or not. It looked like she'd miss the performance until God sent the Ballylumford power workers out on strike. As a result, no one in Northern Ireland got to see *Songs of Praise* that day, and since it was of local interest, BBC Northern Ireland decided to transmit it on the following Wednesday.

Mrs Lawson would beam at this point.

"So with God's will, I did get to see my daughters on the television."

Lunch was early on the day of the prize-giving to allow enough time to prepare the canteen for the buffet. It meant there was time for playing out in the playground. I should have been sensible. Done something ultra-safe like sitting quietly in the shelter or playing one of the clapping games. But it never occurred to me that doing handstands before the prize-giving would cause me any problems on the most important day of my primary school life. Over the years I'd done thousands of them on the grassy patch to the left of the girls' playground. A group of us—Clare, Melanie Cameron, Janet Doherty, Karen Reilly—would often practise there, taking it in turns to decide who was straightest. One moment my legs were soaring straight up, the next I was overbalancing, toppling over and landing hard on my back. I was stunned for a moment, the breath knocked out of me. My back really hurt.

"Shall I go and get Mrs Smith?" Clare said. Mrs Smith was the playground supervisor.

"No, no," I said. "I'll be all right." Slowly I got to my feet, checking that everything was still intact, gently touching my back, rubbing my elbow that had cushioned the fall. It looked like I was going to be OK, no harm done. But then Clare said, "Oh, Constance, look at your shirt."

I twisted my arm round—a sharp green grass stain leapt out from my right-hand sleeve, the one I'd be offering to the governor of the Honourable the Irish Society in little more than an hour.

"Oh no," I said. "Oh no, oh no. How am I going to get this clean?"

I went to seek advice from Mrs Smith. She was the original glass-half-empty woman, but she was all I'd got.

"Oh, you'll not get that out," she said with certainty. "Not without boiling it. No, no chance."

"But I've got the prize-giving this afternoon," I said.

"Well, you should have thought of that before you started ligging about."

As I'd expected, no help. But then I had an idea. "Can I go home, please? I've got a clean shirt there. It's only five minutes' walk from here. I'll be back in plenty of time for the prize-giving."

"Oh, I don't know about that. That would be most irregular."

"Please," I begged. "You know how important it is to Miss Millington that we all look clean and smart. Please. It'll only take me fifteen minutes. I'll be back by ten past one, quarter past by the latest."

In the end she agreed.

"Make sure you change into your outdoor shoes. I've never agreed with those plimsolls. Probably caused your accident in the first place, those plimsolls did."

I should have ignored this instruction. She'd never have

been any the wiser. But at heart I *was* a good girl, so I did what I was told. It was another mistake.

It was hard to run in my clumpy shoes, and I half went over on my ankle a couple of times. But within five minutes I was back home. The house was empty. I let myself in, ignoring the dogs for once—"I've no time," I shouted apologetically—as I sprinted past them up to my bedroom.

I was half undoing my pinafore as I stumbled along the upstairs landing. I flung open the wardrobe door and started riffling through the hanging clothes: Sunday dresses, jeans, a couple of tartan shirts, a jacket. No school shirt.

"It's got to be here."

I went through them again. Still no shirt. I started searching through Joanna's clothes. Still no shirt.

"No, no, no," I started saying over and over again. "Where is it? Where is it?"

I was half sobbing.

Surely my mum would have washed it by now. I usually had a clean shirt on Monday and Wednesday. I was wearing Monday's. Surely the one for Wednesday had been washed.

I raced from my bedroom, leaping down the stairs and out into the covered yard where the washing machine was housed. On top of it was the cream plastic bath that I used to play in as a little girl. It was full of laundry. Dirty laundry. And amongst it was my other white shirt.

I wanted to bite and tear it, let the rage that was boiling inside me rip right through it. But instead I shut my eyes and swallowed hard.

"I just need to calm down," I said to the dogs, who stayed in the covered yard when we were out. "Then I'll be able to think."

I retrieved the shirt. It wasn't too grubby, except round the collar, but it was extremely crumpled. I couldn't wear it in its current state, but although I'd been boiling water since I was six and frying sausages from eight, I'd never used the iron.

I was terrified of the iron. It was Jonathan Duffy's fault. Well, maybe fault is a bit harsh, but my fear of irons could be traced directly to sitting next to Jonathan Duffy in primary 1. His right hand was crumpled and scarred from where he'd placed his open palm on a hot iron while his mother's attention was somewhere else. According to Jonathan, the iron had stuck fast to his flesh. He'd tried to pull his hand away when he felt the scorching heat on his skin but it was too late. It had stuck almost instantaneously. His mother must have been horrified when she heard his screams and turned to see her three-year-old son welded to the iron.

And ever since then I'd been terrified of irons, never turned my back on one, just in case. There was no way that I was plugging in that iron. Not for my parents, not for Miss Millington, not for the Honourable the Irish Society. And especially not for a crumpled shirt that wasn't even clean.

Fifteen minutes had already ticked quickly by since I'd arrived home. In another fifteen I needed to be sitting in the assembly hall with the rest of the prizewinners. I went into the kitchen and from the cupboard under the sink got out the cracked lump of soap that my mother used on difficult stains.

I slipped out of my shirt and quickly wet the grass stain. I rubbed some soap in and scrubbed the material back and forth against itself. Then a little more water and a little more soap and more scrubbing. Finally more and more water to remove the soap. The grass stain was a lot less noticeable, but the sleeve of the shirt was sopping wet. I squeezed it out with all my might.

It was almost half past one by now. I should have been taking my seat in the hall. Instead I was dashing upstairs to spend five minutes attempting to dry the sleeve with the hair dryer in my parents' bedroom. It was still damp when I slipped it on, but I hoped it would be nearly dry by the time of my first appearance on stage.

I splashed some cold water on my face, dried it on the towel and then left the house. I walked quickly back to school and was in my seat by 1.45. Mrs Lawson raised an eyebrow as she saw me slip in, but no one said anything. My sleeve was drying well. Everything was going to be OK.

A few minutes later I saw my mother come in. She made her way carefully to sit with the other parents. She was wearing a pale blue dress that she'd bought in the clothes shop where she worked. Her hair was freshly brushed and her lipstick newly applied. I was pleased to see her, relieved that she was on time. I gave her a small smile, which she returned.

I looked back towards the door, expecting to see my father. But there was no sign of him. Maybe they were coming separately. He'd better get his skates on. I kept glancing from my watch to the door. By one minute to two, he'd still not appeared.

"Where is he?" I thought. "He's going to be late."

I heard the cheers outside which signalled the arrival of the Honourable the Irish Society. Soon I was witnessing for the last time Miss Millington's entrance with her guests.

Still my father hadn't turned up. I couldn't decide which was more humiliating: him arriving late and interrupting the entire performance, or him not coming at all, showing the world how little I mattered.

A moment later my dad was pushed out of my mind. Miss Millington and the governor of the Irish Society had said their opening words, and she was now calling forward class prizes, primary 3a. Which meant that we were all on the move, being sucked row upon row nearer to the front and our own appearance on stage. And that's when I realised I was still wearing the clumpy shoes.

Oh God. What am I going to do?

The primary 3 prizewinners passed in a blur in front of me as I contemplated Miss Millington's face when I clump, clump, clumped across the stage. I'd been so distracted by the grass stain that I'd completely forgotten to change back into my plimsolls. How could I have been so stupid?

I forced myself to stay sitting upright, but all I wanted to do was slump forward till my head hit the comforting barrier of the chair in front. I could just lie there, let it all wash over me, let it all go. It was over, it was finished. None of it had mattered after all. He hadn't come. Why hadn't I realised he wouldn't come? And now I was sitting there in the wrong shoes.

Miss Millington had finished primary 3, 4 and 5. I didn't even remember moving, but I was in the right seat so I must have. Only primary 6 to go. She was calling them now. Time to get a grip. What you can't get over, you have to get through. As we moved forward to the front row, I practised walking as quietly as I could. But it didn't help much. My shoes were still clumping.

And then I heard Miss Millington saying: "And now we come to the highlight of our annual prize-giving. The announcement of the Top Six. The six children who, through their hard work and natural talent, combined with the best teaching this side of the Bann, have achieved so much in which we can all take pride. They are an example to every child in this school and indeed to every one of us. It is my very great pleasure to call those six children forward now."

I rose from my seat and made my way to the top of the steps. Miss Millington announced, "First prize: Constance McCullagh."

The audience clapped as I strode out across the stage to the governor. I gave my best-ever curtsy and a strong, distinct "Thank you". I even answered a couple of questions on my favourite subjects before departing the stage with my atlas. I made my way to the seat that had been saved for me amongst the specialist prizewinners, having carefully dropped off the atlas en-route at a pre-rehearsed spot at the side of the hall.

A couple of minutes later I was back on stage, receiving a geography prize, along with Paul Blane, Janet Mooney and Jack Kennedy. And a minute later I was back again for the Mary Nesbitt Memorial Prize for English. In between, Clare had received her religious education prize.

It was on to arts and crafts. The flush of adrenaline that had got me through the first three prizes faded somewhat as I waited for Miss Millington to get through to primary 7 knitting, which I'd won with a pale-blue tank top.

I wondered if my mother had known he wasn't coming. Wondered how she felt. I'd seen her sitting with the other parents as I'd made my way down the hall to my arts and crafts seat. She was the only one with an empty chair next to her.

Soon the prize-giving was over. After the national anthem, the Top Six were called outside for photos in front of the main entrance with Miss Millington and the governor. I wanted to go and change my shoes first, but the photographer said he didn't have time. I could only hope he'd go for a view from the waist up.

At last I got to change my shoes, and then I joined the guests in the canteen for afternoon tea. My mother was already there. I was impressed but a little anxious to see that she was talking to the governor. But he was laughing, so I guessed she was saying the right things. I loved meringue and helped myself to a piece of pavlova, a pudding that I'd never heard of, let alone eaten before. It was delicious.

I was relaxing at last. But then Fiona McMillan's mother came over.

"Congratulations, Constance," she said to me. She smiled with her lips but her eyes stayed hard. "You must have her working all the hours God sends, Maisie," she said to my mother.

"Oh, no," my mum replied. "I'm not one of these pushy parents. It's just sheer natural ability with Constance."

Mrs McMillan changed tack.

"So where's Victor today? He's the only parent not here. Is he not well?"

My mother should have lied, but instead she said, "No, unfortunately he had to work."

"Work? Oh, I see," she said. "Of course, Brian made sure that he got the day off. He wouldn't have missed Fiona's big day for the world."

I'd never liked Mrs McMillan nor her prissy daughter Fiona. At that moment I wanted to stab her.

"Oh well, I suppose we've all got different priorities," she said, as she sauntered back to Brian and Fiona.

"Let's go," I said to my mother. "The Irish Society will be going in a minute anyway. I heard the governor say that they'd an appointment in Londonderry at six."

I collected my prizes from the cloakroom where I'd stored them. I walked silently home with my mother. I hated Mrs McMillan. But I hated my father more. When we got home I went upstairs to get changed, taking my prizes with me.

"Why don't you leave those downstairs for your father to see when he comes in?" she said.

"If he'd wanted to see them, he'd have come to the prize-giving," I answered.

"Come on now, Constance," she said. "I explained. He couldn't get the time off work."

"All of the other fathers work and they all got the time off. You work, but you made sure you were there. He was the only one, Mummy. The only one not there. He's shown me up and he's shown you up. He's not seeing my prizes."

I went into my bedroom and hid my books under the bed. Then I changed into my jeans and a T-shirt, tied a jumper round my waist.

"I'm taking the dogs out for a walk," I told my mother when I came back down. "I'll probably not come back for tea as I'm stuffed from the buffet."

"I'm really proud of you, Constance. And your grandparents are, too. Try and remember that."

"I'll see you later," I answered.

We went down through the fields to the river. I'd always loved it down there. The tide was in, and I skimmed stones while the dogs went scenting off after rabbits they would never catch. Eventually I sat, watching the sunlight sparkling off the water. The dogs came and lay beside me. We sat there for ages, the water lapping away the worst of my pain. And I decided that that was it. He was never going to hurt me again. From now on he just wasn't going to matter.

When we got home, my father had already been and gone. I was glad. I fed the dogs, then watched TV for a while. I went to bed early, slipping in between the cool sheets. I got my sports cup out, stroking the shiny silver, looking at the names of the previous winners, etched around the base. Then the books, opening them carefully to read the inscriptions inside. Finally the envelope of my knitting prize—£2.50. I wondered what I might buy.

Chapter 12

A Belfast Holiday

CLARE ALWAYS WENT to Donegal for the whole of July, which sometimes left me at a bit of a loose end. But in 1977 I, too, went away in July, to stay with my grandparents in Belfast. I was looking forward to it.

We drove up on a Sunday, dropping my brother off at the airport en route. He was off to work in Rügen, an island off the north coast of Germany, for the summer. Having seen Simon off, it was two o'clock by the time we got to my grandparents'. The door was answered not by either of my grandparents but by Uncle George.

Everyone in the family loved George Wray. He could talk the hind legs off a donkey, and you were sure of a few laughs if he was around. He was always immaculate, never a hair out of place, never a smear or spot on his clothes, blue eyes twinkling and a smile never far from his lips. Like most of my mother's family, he worked in Gallaher's cigarette factory. He hated it.

"All right, Maisie, Victor. How's about ye?"

"Ah, George. I didn't know you were stopping by. You're looking well," my mother replied.

"Thanks. I may be looking well but I've been off my work this past fortnight."

My grandfather laughed. "Wimbledon fever, was it?" he said.

Uncle George always seemed to be ill for Wimbledon fortnight. Sometimes it would be a terrible summer flu that he just couldn't shake or perhaps awful stomach pains so he couldn't stand, let alone work, or else his back would be playing up.

"Och, Uncle Michael, you're a hard man. I've been really bad this time. Industrial injury. They were happy to give me the time off. Insisted I stay off till I felt up till it again."

"What happened you?" my mum asked.

"Well, Maisie, someone had left a bit of piping lying about after fixing one of the machines. Sure I never seen it when I was shifting one of the big boxes of tobacco, and I tripped and fell really badly. It was that bad I was knocked out. First I knew was when I came to with the foreman hanging over me."

"Oh, George, that's terrible."

"Well, I was lucky. I fell forward. If I'd gone to the right, I'd've been in the rolling machine."

"Dear God. Surely they should have better safety."

"Well, that's what the union said. They're looking for compensation for me. So, Uncle Michael, it was nothing to do with Wimbledon. Mind you, it was lucky for me it was Wimbledon time. I've needed something to take me mind off the terrible pain I've been in."

My granda looked shamefaced. "Ah, I'm sorry there, George."

"So you should be. So you should be."

"Is there anything I can do?" my granda said, helpless.

But then my Aunt Roberta started to laugh.

"Come on now, George. Put your Uncle Michael out of his misery," she said.

"Shut up, Roberta," hissed George.

"Ah, George. You've got to come clean, here at least," she said.

"What are you talking about, Roberta?" said my granda.

Roberta laughed again. "Well, Michael, it's like this. He was on his way to work and he thought his hair was out of place—you know how he's always been about his hair?"

"I do, aye," said my granda. "Sure he used to get a special pass to leave Gallaher's early on a Friday afternoon to get himself ready to see you in the evening."

"Well, he was worrying about his hair and was trying to catch his reflection in the window of the barber's, down by Norse Street. Sure, didn't he fall his length over a bit of guttering that had been left lying in the street. Anyway, he picked himself up and limped into work, made sure no one had seen him come in, and then faked his industrial injury at Gallaher's."

Roberta was laughing hard by now. George was staring straight into the fire like he wished it would swallow him up.

"I'll just come and help you make a wee cup of tea, Aunt Peggy," he said.

He leant across and whispered to my Aunt Roberta, "That's the last time I tell you anything." Then he got up, gathering what little dignity he had left about him, and departed to the relative sanctuary of the scullery.

He emerged ten minutes later with a tray of cakes and biscuits, and then with a glass of orange juice for me and cups of tea for everyone else. My granda was keen to bait him about the industrial injury, but my mother came to George's rescue and changed the subject. She'd always had a soft spot for my Uncle George.

Strictly speaking, he wasn't my uncle but my mother's first cousin, only child of my granda's sister Lizzie and her husband Willy Wray. Willy Wray was a legend in the family. He'd been part of the British Expeditionary Force trapped by the advancing Germans on the beaches at Dunkirk. Willy didn't make it to the evacuating boats or into the listings of the prisoners of war taken from the beach. Lizzie received the telegram that every war wife dreaded: "Missing in action, presumed dead".

It was a terrible blow to Lizzie, left to bring up George, their two-year-old son, on her own. On the first anniversary of Dunkirk, she put an "In Memoriam" notice in the paper:

> Willy Wray 1910–1940
> Beloved husband of Lizzie
> And father of George
> His willing hands will toil no more.

There were a few people in the area who raised their eyebrows at the choice of tribute: Willy was always a bit of a chancer, a funny and warm man to be sure, but never known to put in more than the minimum required. A butcher by trade, he'd spend his time chatting with the customers, leaving others to heft the carcasses out the back. Still, he was Lizzie's husband and it was up to her how she chose to remember him.

She stayed living in the house in Spamount Street that she'd shared with Willy and set about slowly rebuilding her life. Her brothers, Jackie and Tommy, lived nearby and would pop in on the way back from work to keep her company.

When George was four, she took a job in the Grove Public Baths. With most people living in small two-up, two-down terraces, the public baths were somewhere to get a proper wash. Lizzie liked her job and settled into a routine, which revolved around work, her son and her family. And so it seemed set to continue.

Until one day in early July 1945 she heard a loud knock on her front door. She'd not been home from work long, George was with Tommy's wife Sadie and wouldn't be home for another thirty minutes, and she had been looking forward to a little rest.

Reluctantly she pushed herself out of her comfy chair and went to open the door. A man in the uniform of the British army stood with his back to her looking up and down the street.

"Hello, can I help you?" she asked.

She gasped as the soldier turned. Although gaunt and pale, the man in uniform was unmistakably Willy Wray.

"Willy? Willy, is that you?"

She started to cry. He took her in his arms, tears in his own eyes.

"Hush now, darling. Hush now, my Lizzie. Aye, it's me."

They stumbled back into the house.

"But how? How? They told me you were dead."

"No, I'm not dead. I've been in a POW camp in Germany since 1940."

"Not dead," she repeated. "In a camp."

"That's right," he said. "Not dead. In a camp."

She rested in his arms for a moment. And then she thumped him really hard across the back of the head, pulling away from him.

"Why didn't you write?" she shouted at him. "Why the hell did you not write, you bastard, and let me know you were safe?" Then, her voice breaking, "You've no idea what I've been through."

"I wrote and wrote. They mustn't have got through. How could you think I'd not write if I had the chance?"

Now it was Willy pulling away.

Lizzie started to sob. And sob. And sob. And when Sadie arrived with George, she found them both sitting sobbing on the sofa in their front room on Spamount Street.

I loved this story. I'd first heard it from Sadie and had then begged Lizzie to tell me it all over again. My mum would tell it too. Great-Uncle Willy was less forthcoming. He'd spend hours regaling you with stories of going to war, the retreat to Dunkirk, hiding in fields for a week before capture, the POW camp and skinning the guard's cat to make stew. And he'd tease my Great-Aunt Lizzie about his epitaph. He used to look down at his hands and then look up at her and say:

"See them hands, Lizzie. They're still toiling. Still toiling." And he'd laugh.

But on the subject of the afternoon of his return, he refused to be drawn.

Chapter 13

Losing the Library

M<small>Y PARENTS AND</small> sister set off back to Coleraine at about half past five. They'd be back in two weeks. I unpacked my few things in the front bedroom: jeans, shorts, a few T-shirts, a jumper, underwear, pyjamas, a dress for church. I'd also brought my jotter and two of the books I'd won at the school prize-giving a couple of weeks before—*A Girl's Adventure Stories* and *Little Men*.

I'd been saving them up, resisting their daily temptation. I loved books and had been addicted to the library from an early age. My mum and I went every Saturday morning. It was a circular building on two levels on a corner on a slope. Two entrances on opposite sides and different levels made it seem even more magical.

My mother would accompany me to the entrance to the children's library on Circular Road. She'd leave me at the door to make my own way into the delights that lay beyond. Meanwhile, she'd walk on round the corner to Park Street and up the dozen outside steps that led to the adult and reference sections. We'd both savour the very individual pleasure of choosing our books for the week.

My mum would usually go for thrillers, smoking guns, knives or nooses adorning the covers. For myself, Babar the

Elephant was an early love. Then it was myths and fairytales—
from Hans Christian Andersen to Greek and Roman gods
and Celtic legends. And, of course, the usual children's clas-
sics—Enid Blyton, Robert Louis Stevenson, *Pinocchio*.
Whichever one of us finished first would seek out the other
via the internal stairs that linked the two levels.

After my mother started working, I'd go to the library
with Clare on a Saturday morning. Then back home, stopping off only to buy sweets at Tindles' Newsagents. We'd try
to get Mr Tindle to serve us. He allowed you to order two-
ounce amounts so you could get two different types of sweets
for your quarter pound. I'd choose from floral gums and
sherbet pipes, Tom Thumb drops, cherry lips or midget
gems, wine gums, pear drops, pineapple chunks or bonbons.
But Mrs Tindle refused to measure less than a quarter, so
you'd have only one choice.

Sometimes Clare would be busy with her family or didn't
feel like the walk to the library if it was raining heavily. On
those days I'd go on my own. And one such trip spelt the end
of the library for me. It was a particularly wet day in November
1973. I'd called for Clare, but her mum thought the rain was
too heavy for us to be out. But if I didn't walk to the library, I'd
have no books for the week, so off I trudged on my own.

The library was over a mile from Clare's house, and I was
very wet by the time I got there. The rain had been running
off my anorak on to my jeans, which were sodden and heavy.
I hung my wet coat up near the door on one of the little
wooden pegs. Mrs McCluskey, the librarian, smiled at me.

"Terrible weather. Why don't you pop into the toilets and
dry yourself off a bit?"

I did as she suggested and then made my way to the

waiting shelves. I began scanning the shelves for something I'd not yet read. It was difficult, but in the end I found *The Wives of Henry the Eighth*. I added two books I had read before, *The Naughtiest Girl in School* and *Tom's Midnight Garden*.

Joanna had asked me to get her a couple of craft books. She was hoping to make something for my parents for Christmas. I'm not sure why. Her previous effort had been a set of oven gloves with the protection sewn into the wrong side. They had to be worn back to front, locking your hands almost together, and were a danger to use. The crafts section was fairly small, but I thought she'd be happy with the hefty *100 Projects for a Rainy Day*. But getting a second craft book was a struggle. I toyed with *Macramé* and *Let's Make Pickles*. In the end I went for *A Girl's Guide to Knitting*. It had not been taken out for five years, but it was small and light and I'd already got two heavy books plus my Enid Blyton and Philippa Pearce to carry.

I took the books over to the desk and presented my library card. Mrs McCluskey stamped the books and then put them in size order.

"You've got a couple of heavy ones there. Do you think you'll be able to manage?"

"I think so, thank you."

"You've nearly run out of books down here, haven't you? We'll have to start thinking about a ticket for the adult library for you soon. You wouldn't be allowed all the books up there, but there's a lot you could have a go at."

The adult library! I pulled on my damp anorak trying to imagine myself searching the shelves of the adult library. The rain had eased off a little, but the books kept slipping as I struggled along and I kept having to readjust my hold. I stopped on the Old Bridge and put the books on the wall to give my arms a rest. I'd come only a few hundred yards. It was going to be a long journey home. Still, at least I had the prospect of the adult library to keep me going.

Best not stop at Tindles', too much to carry already, I thought to myself.

It was time to get moving again. I reached out to gather up my books. And as I did so, a sudden gust of wind lifted the top book, *A Girl's Guide to Knitting*. I watched horrified as it fluttered down to the river, and then floated away, downstream towards the sea.

Oh God.

I grabbed the four remaining books, ran across the bridge and on to the path alongside the river. I tried to keep up with the book, but it was hopeless. The Bann is a wide, fast-flowing river and was swollen from the heavy rain. The book was floating away, and nothing I could do would get it back.

I stood there watching until it went out of view. What was I going to do? Slowly I turned away from the river and began the long trek home. The rain had come on heavy again and was driving into my face. I stuffed the remaining books up my coat to try to keep them dry.

What was I going to do?

By the time I got home I'd decided to do nothing. I told Joanna I'd been able to get her only one book. I pretended the events on the bridge hadn't happened, pretended *A Girl's Guide to Knitting* out of existence. If no one knew about it, maybe it would go away.

I got my mother to take the surviving books back for me and told her I was sick of reading when she asked if I wanted her to get me some more out. Two weeks later I intercepted a reminder card for *A Girl's Guide to Knitting* from the library. I tore it up and buried the scraps at the bottom of the bin.

That'll fix it, I thought.

The next card was demanding not only the return of the missing book but also a fine for lateness. I crushed it and put it in a litter bin near school. I was really missing my reading by now. But there was nothing to be done about it.

I should have known I couldn't go on destroying the evidence for ever. Lucky for me it was my mother who got the next card. It came on a Thursday, her day off from work. The post had been late that morning, so there had been no chance for me to intercept it.

When I got home from school, she asked me about the card. "It's not like you to have books overdue, Constance. You're going to have to pay a fine. Why don't you go and take it back now?"

I looked down, then back at my mum. I shook my head.

"I can't," I said. "I haven't got it."

"Well where is it?" she said.

It was such a relief to tell her what had happened. She gave me a hug.

"Och, Constance, you should have told me. It wasn't your fault. I'll go in and explain. I'm sure they'll understand."

"What about Daddy?"

"What about him?"

"Are you going to tell him?"

"No, there's no reason to involve him. Don't worry now. Why don't you go and get changed, and I'll cut us both a slice of caramel shortbread. We can sit down and watch the telly for a while."

She went to the library the next day during her lunch hour. She told me Mrs McCluskey was very understanding and waived the fine.

"She said to be sure and tell you to come back again," my mum said.

But I never did.

Chapter 14

The Bonfire

MY FIRST DAY at my grandparents' set a pattern for the week. I got up at about a quarter to eight and joined my grandparents downstairs for a breakfast of cereal and toast. My granda had already been out for the papers—the *Daily Mirror* and *The Sun*. Even though he'd stopped working ten years before, he still rose at six.

We read the papers and then played cards for a while. My granda loved playing cards. He'd been a bit of a gambler in his youth but had quit the day he got married and had never made another bet. But he still loved the cards.

We started off with pontoon. He'd taught me the rules when I was four, and we'd been playing ever since. The cards were stored in the cupboard above his rocking chair. When I was small, I'd sit up in his lap and he'd deal the cards to me. But now, I sat on a little three-legged stool in front of him. It also put me in front of the coal fire. I loved the fire and would happily sit poking it for hours at a time.

We played a few games of pontoon. Then he said, "Do you still want to learn poker?"

I'd been asking for years, but until now he'd been saying I was too young to appreciate it.

"Oh, yeah. I really, really do. Will you teach it to me, Granda?"

"I think you're just about old enough now."

He started by explaining the rules: the role of the dealer, the first deal, how many cards you could change, how to stay in the game, when to get out, what beat what. Then he gave me my chips—burnt matchsticks he'd been saving for the purpose. He said it wasn't really gambling, but that you needed some currency for raising the stakes. And so we started.

We played up until dinner time that first morning. We always had dinner at half twelve, and it was almost always some form of meat and potatoes—cooked ham or sausages with mash, mince and boiled potatoes, champ with corned beef, Irish stew. The only exception was Fridays when it would always be chips and fried peas. Today it was sausages and mash.

Meals were pretty predictable at my grandparents'. Tea was always at half past four and always salad—usually lettuce, tomato, scallions and beetroot with cooked ham or corned beef, sometimes a boiled egg, and a large plate of buttered white bread. I hated salad, but loved sandwiches, so managed all right. At nine o'clock we'd have supper—toast, biscuits and a hot milky drink for my grandparents, orange juice for me. We'd often be in bed within half an hour, by ten at the latest.

I loved my grandparents, but by Thursday I was beginning to feel penned in. I'd been to the Grove Park with my granda for a walk a couple of times and to the shops at the bottom of the road for my granny, but the rest of the time had been spent in my grandparents' front room. I was relieved on Friday when my granda and I went to the Grove Public Baths where my Great-Aunt Lizzie had worked. I got a ticket for the

swimming pool while my granda went to the slipper baths.
My grandparents didn't have a bath, only a Belfast sink in the
scullery, so they went to the Grove for their weekly bath. The
sessions were single sex, so my grandparents went at different times.

I did twenty lengths of the pool, then showered, washed
my hair and got dressed again. My granda was already waiting
when I came out, his gleaming white hair combed back from
his face.

As we were leaving, a thick-set woman with short bleached-
blonde hair, dark roots and a home-carved tattoo of "No sur-
render" on her upper arm spoke to my grandfather.

"Hi there, Mr Linton. How are you doing?"

"Fine, Mandy. Fine. And yourself?"

"Ah, I can't complain," she said.

I couldn't believe that my strait-laced granda knew such a
woman. She looked as if she'd been dragged up.

"Who's this with you?" she said.

"This is our Constance. Maisie's youngest. She's up staying with us for a couple of weeks."

At that moment, a blonde-haired girl came running up to
us.

"Ah, here you are. I was beginning to think someone had
eaten you on the way back," Mandy said.

The girl looked away and tutted under her breath.

"This is our Janice," Mandy said to me. Then, to my
granda, "Halfway here she realises she's forgotten her
costume."

"Well, say hello," Mandy instructed Janice. "This here's
Constance, Mr Linton's granddaughter."

The girl grunted hello; I muttered the same in return.

"Young ones these days, Mr Linton. What are they like? Anyway, we best let you get off," she said. They disappeared into the public baths, and my granda and I set off home.

"Who were they?" I asked as we walked along.

"That was Mandy Wright and Janice," he said.

"But who are they?"

"They live in Crosscollyer Street, the one that runs along the top of Mountcollyer Road, Mountcollyer Avenue and Mountcollyer Street."

"How do you know them?"

"Ah, there's no end to the people I know," he replied and changed the subject to Manchester United. I let myself be diverted. My granda had brought me up a Man U fan, and I enjoyed talking about the season past and discussing our hopes for the new one. But still I was intrigued by Mandy and wanted to know more. I decided to ask my granny. The opportunity came after lunch while my granda was washing up.

"How was swimming?" she asked.

"Good," I replied. "And we met someone when we were coming out. Mandy Wright she was called."

"Oh, yes." My granny was noncommittal.

"Who is she?"

"She lives up in Crosscollyer Street."

"That's what granda said. But who is she?"

"What do you mean?"

"I don't know. She just doesn't seem like the other people you know. She's got bleached hair. And a tattoo."

My granny laughed. "You can't always judge people from the outside. She's a good woman. Raising that child like her own."

"What child? Janice? Is Janice not Mandy's daughter? Who is she, Granny?"

"You're certainly full of questions today. I thought that swim might have worn you out. No, Janice isn't Mandy's real daughter. She was the child of a friend of Mandy's, Esme. Esme got cancer when Janice was only two. There was nothing the doctors could do. Mandy took the pair of them in when it was diagnosed. Esme died in the house above. And Mandy promised her that she'd raise the wee'un."

"So what age is she—Janice?"

"Well now, let me think. It must be this eight years now that she moved here. So she must be about ten. Anyway, enough of the questions. Can you run down to the shop for some ham for the night's tea. And here's a shilling, get yourself a wee sweetie."

It took a little over five minutes to and from the shop. But in that short time, Janice Wright had got herself installed in my granny's front room with a glass of brown lemonade and a plate of assorted biscuits and was laughing away with my granda.

"Ah, here she is now," he said as I returned. "Janice was wondering if you wanted to play with her this afternoon."

I was both excited at the prospect of playing with someone my own age and wary—there was something about Janice I wasn't sure I liked. We set off for the playground talking round the skeletons of our lives: schools, homes, interests. She went to Newington Primary School, just up the road. She lived with her mother (as she referred to Mandy) at 38 Crosscollyer Street. She was a Liverpool fan and gloated at their league triumph.

I expected to play on the usual things like the swings,

the roundabout and the witch's hat. The hat was my favourite—a cone-shaped metal frame with wooden benches round the bottom that pivoted on a solid metal pole. It would judder and swing violently if there were enough of you on it.

But instead she led me to a large heap of junk at the back of the playground. There were two lads about our age hanging around the edge. An older one, who I later found out was Billy, was talking to them.

"We need far more stuff than this," he said. "This is bollox. This is pure fucking bollox. What kind of an eleventh night do youse think we're going to have with this pile of shite? Do youse want the Taigs fucking laughing at you? Laughing their arse off at the poor fucking show from North Queen Street. Let alone the brothers from Sandy Row, from the Shankill, from the Crumlin Road, saying we've let down the Protestant cause."

He carried on, ignoring their attempts to speak.

"So get the fuck out of here. All of youse," and he was including Janice and me by now. "Away and get some more fucking stuff for this here bonfire."

The two lads were Pete, the same age as me, and Johnny, who was twelve. We set off out of the playground.

"Where are we gonna get some stuff?" said Janice.

"My brother, Jonty, he works in a garage," said Pete. "I'm sure we could get some old tyres."

"That would help," Johnny said. "But we need some wood. Where can we get some bastardin' wood?"

We all thought, though given that I'd spent my entire time at my grandparents', I'd not much to contribute. It was Janice who had sudden inspiration.

"You know that house at the bottom of Mountcollye
Avenue? The one that's been empty this past few weeks? W
might be able to get stuff there."

We all agreed that this was a great plan and set off t
Mountcollyer Avenue. As with all of the Mountcollyer street
there was an upper and a lower part, divided by North Quee
Street. The house in question was in the lower section. I
doors and windows had been boarded up by the Corpora
tion. We tried with our hands, but there was no way of for
ing the planks off, and we did not want to draw attention t
ourselves by hanging around there for too long.

We decided to have a go from round the back and quic
ly made our way to the entry and up to the house. It didn
take long for Pete and Johnny to get the old entry doo
which was half rotten, off its hinges. The back windows wer
boarded, but Johnny popped home for his father's tools, an
we soon had the first plank prised off. And then another. An
another. Within ten minutes we were inside the house. It wa
dark and thrillingly creepy. There was no furniture and ha
the floorboards were missing.

"I bet them bastards from Deacon Street have alread
been here," said Johnny.

Deacon Street was another Protestant street a bit furthe
down North Queen Street, where my Granny McCullagh ha
lived until she went into the old people's home.

"Or maybe even them ones from up the Limestone Roa
Could have been the bastard that got fried." A few days earl
er a lad had been badly burned after the bonfire junk he'
been guarding overnight got set alight early in the mornin

We made our way across the joists and through the ope
doorway. A few boards remained in the front room and th

stairs were still intact. We went upstairs—neither bedroom had been touched. As well as the floorboards, there was an old chest of drawers in one room.

"This is fuckin' fantastic," said Pete. "What a great idea, Janice."

Pete and Johnny set about taking up the floorboards in the front bedroom. Meanwhile, Janice and I dragged the chest of drawers to the top of the stairs. It was too heavy to carry, so we pushed it down the stairs. It crashed at the bottom and split apart with a huge bang. We held our breaths. There was no sound from the houses next door. We stood still for another minute, but no one came. So we made our way downstairs. Now that it was broken we were able to carry the chest of drawers, though it took us two journeys.

By the time we returned, a small pile of floorboards had already accumulated. We began journeying back and forth between the house and the playground, carrying a few planks at a time. As the afternoon wore on, more and more kids joined in, stripping the wood out of the house like locusts. The time flew by, and too soon it was time for me to be going home for tea. There was a water fountain near the entrance to the playground. I did my best with a wet hankie to clean the dirt off my face and hands and managed to make it through the door just as the first of the cuckoo clocks chimed for half past four.

I wanted to go out again after tea, but my granda said no. I did sneak a peek out of the back bedroom window when I went upstairs to get *A Girl's Adventure Stories*. But only the front of the playground was visible from the window; the rear with the precious bonfire was hidden by the angle of the entry wall. I gave up and settled myself back downstairs with my book.

At about half six there was a knock at the door. My granda shouted, "Come in."

It was Janice, asking if I could come out to play. My hopes rose, but my granda said, "Not tonight, love. She's booked to play cards with me instead. You can join us if you like."

"Ah no, Mr Linton," she replied. "You're all right."

"Suit yourself."

"I'll call for you tomorrow," she said to me as she made her way back out the front door.

The next day I rose as usual at 7.45 a.m. and joined my grandparents downstairs. I played cards after breakfast, and then my granda suggested a walk to the Grove Park. I didn't want to hurt his feelings so I agreed. We passed the playground on the way. The bonfire pile had really grown since I'd left it the previous afternoon. It was only nine o'clock, but a couple of young lads were already engaged in bringing more wood. Billy was there directing. He waved in our direction. I waved back.

"How do you know him?" asked my granda.

"I met him yesterday in the playground with Janice."

"Keep you away from him. Do you hear me? Keep you away. That family's trouble."

"What do you mean, Granda? What's he done?"

"Never you mind what he's done. But just you heed what I'm telling you."

There was no point questioning my granda. As far as he was concerned, the conversation was over. We stayed an hour in the park and then headed back to Mountcollyer Road. As we passed the playground, I spotted Janice playing on one of the swings near the entrance.

"Hello, Mr Linton. Can Constance come and play again today?"

"We're busy this morning," he replied. "But she'll see you after her dinner."

I spent the rest of the morning with my granda and his friend Wilfie Simmons. Wilfie lived just off the Limestone Road and kept pigeons. He talked more to the pigeons than to either my granda or me. I've never been that keen on pigeons, and it was a relief when my granda suggested we go home.

After dinner I helped clear away the dishes and then asked if it was OK to go and play with Janice. My granda nodded his agreement, and I set off happily for the playground. I spent the afternoon rolling used tyres from Pete's brother's garage to the bonfire and helping rearrange the pile so it was fairly stable.

As before, the time whizzed by, and soon it was back to my grandparents' for tea. Janice dropped in on her way home. We played pontoon for a while with my granda and then she took her leave.

"Will you be coming out tomorrow?" she asked me.

"No, not tomorrow," my granda said.

"Ah, but Mr Linton, we're making the effigy tomorrow. She can't miss that."

"Who are you doing? Lundy or the Pope?" he asked.

Almost 300 years on from the siege of Derry, Lundy was still a figure of hate for most loyalists. But my granda would always go for the Pope, the antichrist incarnate. He hated Catholicism with an almost phobic intensity. "They're plotting while you're sleeping," he'd often say, or "It's not a religion, it's a disease."

"The Pope," replied Janice.

My granda was delighted. "Well, make sure you do a good job," he said.

"So can she come?" Janice said.

"What?" My granda was momentarily confused. "No, no I already said. She's got other things on tomorrow. She'll see you on Monday."

Chapter 15

Sinclair Seamen's

THE NEXT DAY I went with my granda to his church, Sinclair Seamen's, a thirty-minute walk away in central Belfast. I put on the pale blue dress I'd brought with me, the first time I'd been out of trousers all week. I hated all dresses and skirts, except for my school uniform. My trainers were replaced by a pair of hideous, black patent-leather sling-back shoes that I'd inherited from my sister. My granny offered to do my hair, but I was worried my mum had learned her vicious approach at her own mother's knee, so I brushed it myself. It was fairly short so I managed OK without the need for any fuss.

The walk to church was pure purgatory. My sling-backs didn't fit very well, and I kept tripping or going over on my ankle every few yards. To begin with, my granda thought this was funny, but by the end of a two-mile walk, the joke had worn thin even for him.

We arrived at church in plenty of time—unlike my mother, my granda was never late—and took a seat in his usual pew. It was a beautiful church, originally associated with seamen from the nearby docks. The pulpit was in the form of the prow of a ship, the collection boxes were shaped like lifeboats and one of the stained-glass windows showed a ship being tossed on a stormy sea. From the ceiling hung an array of old flags from merchant and battle ships.

After the service my granda paused to talk to an old friend, Jimmy Leighton.

"How's about you, Jimmy?"

"I can't complain, Michael. Can't complain. And yourself?"

"Not bad."

"I heard your Jack wasn't doing too well. How is he?"

"Oh, Michael, he's not good. Not good at all."

"Tell him I was asking for him, will ye?"

"I will. I'm sure you'll be marching on Tuesday."

"I will, if God spares me. But I don't think I'll make it all the way to the field." The twelfth of July march in Belfast always went to the field in Edenderry, on the outskirts of south Belfast. "It's a bit far for me these days. I think I'll be in one of the cars for part of the way. We're getting on, aren't we, Jimmy?"

"Aye, Michael, that we are. Well, I hope to see you on Tuesday."

My granda was quiet to begin with on the journey back from church. But when we got to York Road, he said, "Did I ever tell you about a man that lived near here who had a lion?"

"Oh, was that Buck Alec? Did you know him, Granda?"

I'd heard about Buck Alec from my mum. We were watching *Ben Hur* the first time she mentioned him.

"Victor," she said, "do you remember us going to this when we were courting?"

My father made no response. Undeterred, she continued, "Ah, you must remember. Sure wasn't Buck Alec parading up and down outside with his lion?" She laughed. "Your

Gertrude near took the head-staggers when she seen the beast. I'll never forgot the look on her face." She laughed again.

"Was it a real lion?" I said.

"Aye," my mother answered. "Big brute of a thing it was, with the mane and everything."

"Was it from a zoo or a circus?" I asked.

"I don't know where he got it from, but he had it like a pet. Kind of."

"If you two are going to chitter like bloody budgies, would you take yourselves off somewhere else. I'm trying to listen to the film," my father said.

We fell silent. My dad had been in a good mood all day, and it wasn't worth spoiling it. My mum and I went through to the kitchen to make some tea and biscuits and continue our conversation.

"Where did it live? Did he have a cage in the garden? It must have been a big garden."

"A garden? He lived in a house the same as your granda, two-up, two-down, with a small yard out the back. The lion stayed in the yard during the day. The coal man wouldn't deliver—left the coal in the alley for Buck Alec to take in himself."

"But wasn't that cruel? A lion would need more space than a wee yard."

"Sure, he took it out on a lead. It used to clear the street."

I'd seen exotic animals in the Causeway Safari, and I'd heard stories of people who had wild animals as pets, big cats in a fenced-off area of the back garden. But in the tiny yard of a terraced house and exercised on a lead through the streets of Belfast—this was something else.

"And where did it sleep? Did it have a kennel?"

"I heard tell it slept in the house. The lion downstairs, his children upstairs in one bedroom, and him and the wife in the other bedroom. How she slept I don't know. I'd've been worried out of my mind about the lion getting to the children in the night."

After that first discussion, my mother would often refer to Buck Alec, if my father was doing something ridiculous. She'd lean over, out of my father's earshot, and say, "What's he like? Parading about like Buck Alec without the lion."

"Who's been telling you about Buck Alec?" my granda asked.

"Mummy."

"Well, you probably know everything about him already, then," he said.

"Oh, no, Granda," I said. "Hardly anything. Please, tell me more. Please."

He laughed. "All right then. It was on this very corner that I saw the lion for the first time. I was on my way to work, when I heard this roar from up ahead. I looked up and could hardly believe my eyes. A full-grown lion on a lead not even twenty yards away."

"Oh, were you frightened, Granda?"

"Well, to be honest, at the time I was too shocked to be scared."

"Was it pulling and straining?"

"No, apart from that one roar, it walked along very calm."

"So how did Buck Alec keep it under control? Was he very big and strong?"

"Well, now he wasn't that tall. Smaller than me. But I've heard he was strong, a bit of a hard man. But I don't think it was the strength that did it anyway."

"Well, did he have a whip then?"

"No, nothing like that. I don't know exactly how he did it, but I heard tell that he used to just talk softly and croon in his throat to it."

"Does he still have the lion now, Granda?"

"No, love. This is years ago. I think it died before you were even born."

We were nearly home by now.

"I'll get you some new sandals tomorrow," he said. "You can't be going around tripping for ever."

We had our usual Sunday dinner with my granny. I wondered how the bonfire was coming along and what the effigy looked like. Janice didn't call in and I didn't ask to go out. The afternoon ticked by. My granda's house was full of clocks, cuckooing or chiming every fifteen minutes. On a quiet day at home I would have got lost in a book, but my granda never let you have peace to read. My granny would tune him out while she read the deaths listed in the *Belfast Telegraph*, her only hobby. But I couldn't do that. We played ludo for a while.

At three o'clock I went with my granny to what she called "the meeting": Bible readings, prayers and a few hymns in a small community hall near by. But the route didn't take us past the playground, so I couldn't check on progress. My granda had our salad tea laid out when we got back. Afterwards we returned to the front room for more quiet contemplation. At last the TV was switched on for the news and *Songs of Praise*. The TV helped pass the time, but even so, I went to bed early, slipping quickly to sleep.

Chapter 16

Eleventh Night

O N MONDAY I couldn't wait to get down to the play-ground, but instead I set off to the city centre with my granda to get some new shoes. It was a security zone with bag searches and metal-detector scans in all of the large stores. There were security gates on every entrance to the city cen-tre, and everyone was subject to body searches. We arrived at the gates at ten to nine. There were about half a dozen people, some in shop uniforms, ahead of us in two queues—one male, one female—waiting to be searched. I joined the women's queue while my granda joined the men's.

"Hey, wee lad," one of the women said to me, "you're in the wrong queue." My face burned. I was a bit of a tomboy, but I hated it when people mistook me for a boy. It was par-ticularly humiliating in women's toilets.

"I'm a girl," I said.

The woman laughed. "My mistake, love," she said.

I scowled and looked away. I could see my granda already through the barriers and waiting for me on the other side. I stood with my arms up and feet apart while the security guard ran her hands over me. Finding nothing of concern, she allowed me through.

We reached British Home Stores, first stop on my

granda's itinerary, just as the doors were opening. We were the only customers. We went straight to the children's department, but it turned out they didn't sell shoes. My granda gave the shop assistant a look that could have coffined her and turned on his heel with me trailing in his wake. We repeated the same performance at C&A.

"Where does your mother get you shoes?" he asked me.

"Trainers come from the catalogue, school shoes from Bishop's in Coleraine. They've got assistants who measure your feet so you get the right size."

"Ah, what do they know? Your mother persuaded me to be measured for shoes a few years ago, and they said I needed an eight when I've always taken a ten. Anyway I took the eights as they suggested, and sure didn't they near cripple me. I could barely put one foot in front of the other."

The size tens that my granda wore were clearly too big—you could see for yourself a huge gap between his heel and the back of his shoes when he walked along—but there was no point arguing with him, so I said nothing. In the end we went to Clarks and he bought me a pair of sensible flat black lace-ups that I could also wear to school. I wasn't sure I liked them, but I knew my granda wouldn't want me trying on the range of options. It was only 9.25 a.m. but he was already anxious that we'd be washed away by a tide of mid-morning shoppers. We proceeded to Marks and Spencer, bought the few things my granny wanted, including Scotch pies for lunch, and were home just after ten.

I'd not been back long when Janice called and asked if I wanted to help set up for the street party. There was usually a children's street party around the twelfth of July. Since Christmas, Mandy Wright had been collecting money each week from every household in Mountcollyer Avenue, Road and Street and Crosscollyer Street, to pay for it.

A number of the women and older girls were already setting up trestle tables down the middle of the street when we arrived in Mountcollyer Avenue. Janice and I were set to taping alternating Union Jack and bright orange plastic tablecloths on to the trestles. As with Mountcollyer Road, the Union Jack or Red Hand of Ulster hung from the upper floor of all of the houses. Many, like my granda, had a metal holster fitted for the purpose. Lines of red, white and blue bunting added to the festive air.

"How's the bonfire been coming along?" I asked Janice, as we worked our way along the tables.

"You should see it now. It's massive. Far bigger than the ones in Deacon Street and the Limestone Road. Billy's done a grand job. There's no messing with him on the case."

"No," I said. "He's a bit fierce."

"If you think he's bad, you should meet his brother."

"Will he be here today?"

"Not much chance of that. He's in Long Kesh." Long Kesh was one of Northern Ireland's high-security prisons.

"What's he in for?"

"Life. Though Billy says he'll be out in fifteen."

"No. I meant what did he do? To get locked up?"

"Murder," she replied. "Shot three Catholics outside a chippie. Mind you, they say he done a lot more than that, but they didn't have the evidence."

Mandy Wright came up to us.

"Can you girls come and help bringing out the food? Go there with Mrs Welch and she'll tell you what to do."

Mrs Welch was a large, slow-moving, somewhat breathless

woman in her late fifties. As we walked up the gentle incline of Mountcollyer Avenue, she panted instructions to us.

"We'll . . . start . . . with the . . . sausages. They're up . . . in Mandy's."

We brought out tray upon tray of cocktail sausages, laying them at intervals down the length of the tables. Then it was chicken legs from Mrs Doherty and sausage rolls from Mrs McLure and sandwiches and sandwiches and sandwiches from Mrs McDermott, Mrs Palmer and Mrs McAfee. We added big bowls of crisps and smaller ones of nuts. As we worked, someone set up a record player by their front door, and soon it was blasting out the loyalist hit parade.

"We're up to our necks in Fenian blood, So come on shout hurray," brought the women to life, especially on the chorus of "We are, we are, we are the Billy Boys." By the time of the loyalist anthem, "The Sash", they were singing and swaying along with the music:

It is old but it is beautiful and the colours they are fine;
It was worn at Derry, Aughrim, Enniskillen and the Boyne.
Oh, my father wore it as a lad in bygone days of yore,
And it's on the twelfth I love to wear
the sash my father wore.

The music had brought other people out on to the street, and soon we were taking our places at the tables. The children sat on the top two-thirds, and the adults who were around took up the seats at the bottom. There was lots of laughing and joking at the tables. Everyone was in a good mood.

Eventually the savoury was cleared away and cakes and biscuits were brought out of two of the nearby houses. It was nearly three before people started drifting away.

My grandparents went home while I stayed to help dismantle the tables. We worked quickly and were finished in less than an hour. Janice and I decided to nip round to the playground for a look at the bonfire. It was massive, maybe thirty foot high and forty foot across. It was made up mostly of tyres and wood. I could see parts of the old chest of drawers that Janice and I had taken from the empty house. Tied against a wooden post at the top was the figure of the Pope.

"What time are they lighting it?" I asked.

"About half nine."

"I hope my granda will let me out for it."

There were a lot of lads in the playground. They were taking it in turns to hurl sticks spinning high up into the air and then trying to catch them. This was a skill that those leading out the loyalist bands on the twelfth had to perfect, but all the lads liked to have a go.

I left Janice talking to Pete and Johnny and headed back to my grandparents'. Even though the party had finished only an hour and a half before, we were still having tea at the usual time. I squeezed down a slice of ham with some salad and two pieces of bread. While I was helping clear up, the door knocked. It was Janice asking if I could come out. To my surprise, my granda agreed but said I had to be back by 8.30.

"But she'll miss the lighting of the bonfire, Mr Linton."

"You wee girls can't be running around on your own when it's getting late."

"We won't be on our own," Janice said. "My mum will be there. From nine o'clock anyway."

He thought for a minute.

"OK then. But I want you back by half ten."

"Oh, thanks, Granda," I said. "Thanks a lot. I'll see you later." I made towards the front door, but my granny called me back.

"Go you upstairs and get an extra jumper," she said. "It'll get cold later, and I don't want you catching a chill."

I tied the jumper round my waist and set off with Janice. We whiled away the next few hours in and around the playground doing nothing in particular. At about a quarter to nine, we went up to Crosscollyer Street to get Mandy Wright, and then the three of us made our way down to the bonfire. It was a dry evening and still light; it would be at least another hour before darkness would draw in.

There were quite a few people already scattered around the playground when we arrived, and the crowd quickly thickened as the time approached for lighting the fire. I saw Pete with a young man in his late teens who I presumed was his brother Jonty. He smiled and then came over.

"Hi," he said. "Looking forward to getting it lit?"

A woman who'd been helping out at the party came over next. While she was talking to Janice and Mandy, Pete said to me in a low voice, "Here, these are for you." He opened his hand to reveal two Highland toffee chews and three blackjacks.

"I know they're not much," he said, "but I wanted you to know I like you."

"Thanks," I said, taking them. "Thanks a lot. Highland toffee's my favourite."

"See you," he said, and sauntered off to rejoin his brother.

I stuck the sweets in my pocket.

"What was that about?" asked Janice.

"Oh, nothing," I said.

"I think they're about to light it," Mandy said. "Here comes Billy with the torch." I followed her gaze to Billy, making his way through the crowd, a flaming torch held high above his head.

"For God and Ulster," he shouted, thrusting the torch into our carefully assembled creation. He walked round the fire, igniting the rags soaked in petrol, which had been placed all around it. The fire took very little time to take a hold, and soon the wood was starting to burn. It took a while before the flames reached the Pope, but as they did a great cheer went up.

Above it, Billy's voice rose, "Death to the Fenians. Death to all traitors."

The smell of burning tyres began to saturate the air. I was glad when it was time to go, Mandy and Janice escorting me to my grandparents' door. They had my supper waiting and we went straight to bed afterwards.

Chapter 17

The Twelfth of July

MY GRANDA WAS up at six the next morning, as usual. I got up soon after and chatted to him as he had a wet shave in the scullery. Afterwards he finished getting dressed: a crisp white shirt over his string vest, tucking it in carefully to his dark suit trousers, then a dark tie. He left his suit jacket hanging by the door, ready for the off. He opened up the cupboard above his rocking chair and got out a parcel wrapped in tissue paper—his Orange Order collarette. It was orange brocade edged with purple and a silvery fringe, and decorated with silver emblems: a crown, an open Bible and a candlestick. It was similar to my father's, except for the different LOL (Loyal Orange Lodge) number and the letters PM, mounted on the right-hand panel.

"What does PM stand for?" I asked.

"Past Master. I used to be master of the lodge."

"Oh. Can I try it on?"

"No. It's not for dressing-up games." He was sharp. Then, softening a little, "But you can lay it out on the cabinet for me."

It was surprisingly heavy. I laid it down carefully.

"Will you be wearing a bowler?" I asked.

"No."

"My da wears a bowler."

"That's up to him. I prefer not."

"What about the white gloves? He wears them as well."

"No. Just my suit and my collar. That'll do me," he said. "It's time for your granny to be up if she wants to see me off. Run upstairs there and waken her, will ye, while I get my breakfast."

I woke my granny and then went to my own room to get dressed. By the time I got back downstairs, my granda had put on his jacket and collar and was unlocking the front door.

"I'll see you tonight," he said to me. "Peggy, I'm off," he shouted up to my granny.

"I'm just coming," she shouted back, clattering down the stairs. Her hair was still in curlers and she'd not yet got her stockings on. She gave him a quick hug and said, "Don't you be walking too much of that route. There's no shame in being in the car at your age."

"Ah, stop fussing now," he said. "I'll do what I do."

With that he was off up the road to join the rest of his lodge gathering in Crosscollyer Street. My granny sat down on the sofa, kicked off her slippers and started pulling on her stockings. Her long pink flannel knickers were briefly revealed as she attached the stockings at the top.

"That's better," she said, sliding her feet back into her slippers. "Now, I wonder, do I have time to do my hair before they pass? Constance, keep you a watch out the front and let me know when they're coming."

I stood out by the front gate, looking up the street. Mr Welch said hello as he passed on his way to join the lodge.

"Will it be long, do you think?" I asked him.

"No, love. We should be marching back down in five minutes, I would think."

I popped in to tell my granny. She'd been removing the curlers and the back of her hair stuck out at strange angles, released but not yet rearranged into my granny's preferred style. She kept her hair fairly short but liked a slight curl to it, though not as much as delivered by a perm. Even though she was seventy-four, it was still fairly dark, with the odd sprinkling of grey on the sides and back. The front was a different story: a thick lock of pure white stood out just to the left of centre.

"Are they coming?" she asked when she saw me.

"No, not yet, but Mr Welch says they'll be no more than five minutes."

"Go on back out and let me know when you actually see them," she said, her hands flying about her hair, whipping out the last few curlers. I can't have been outside more than thirty seconds when the lodge banner appeared in view at the top of the street. It was mounted on two poles, each held in a leather harness by one of the heftier-looking men from the lodge, with cords at either side clutched by two of the younger lads to help keep it straight.

I dashed to the front door and called my granny. Her hair was still far from finished, so she grabbed a headscarf out of the dresser drawer and tied it round her head. The lodge banner was only a few yards away when we arrived on the street. The typical Orange lodge banner depicted King Billy in a hi-ho-Silver pose on the back of a black or white horse. My granda's lodge banner was different; it showed a group of Irish soldiers marching into battle at the Somme. Thousands of Ulstermen died at the Somme and countless others were injured. Nearly every Ulster family had some kind of connection to the battle. One of the few things I knew about my

father's father, William McCullagh, was that he'd managed to
survive the Somme unscathed.

My granny and I weren't the only ones up to see the lodge
off. Women and children standing in front of the houses the
length of the street were clapping as the men came past. I
waved at my granda, and he acknowledged me with a curt
salute and a brief smile.

"Why don't you follow them along the road for a bit?" my
granny said. "They're meeting up with one of the bands and
another lodge at York Road."

"Will you come too?"

"Oh no," she said. "I'll be in the house getting my breakfast. But you go."

"Well, if you don't mind."

I darted along the pavement to catch up and then fell
into step near to my granda. We carried straight across North
Queen Street and then along the lower part of Mountcollyer
Road. At York Road we paused, the men shuffling their feet
and murmuring to each other as we waited for the York Road
Defenders, a loyalist flute band, to make their way up the
road.

The band was led by Johnny, who was walking out in front
with a long blue baton held diagonally across his body. The
band was not playing, but there was a single beat from the
drummers on every second stride. As they approached, they
started to play "Three Cheers for the Red, White and Blue".
It was a young band, mostly twelve- to sixteen-year-olds, but
they held the tune fine. They were dressed in blue trousers,
white shirts, white sweaters, blue bow-ties and blue berets. I
spotted Pete on the far side, playing the flute. He looked well.
As they reached the end of Mountcollyer Road, Johnny

hurled his baton into the air, catching it and twirling it behind him and up over his shoulder.

My granda's lodge fell in behind the band. Further up the road, another lodge was waiting. It slotted in in front of the band, and the three sets of men carried on towards the main parade. I decided to head back home for breakfast with my granny.

We chatted for a while about school. I'd just completed my final year at primary school and would be starting my new school in September. I'd passed my eleven-plus and would be going to the girls' grammar school, Coleraine High, on the other side of town.

The results had come on a Saturday morning in May. My mum came into the bedroom I shared with Joanna to tell me. She didn't make too much of a fuss, in case it made Joanna feel bad, but when I popped in to see her in the shop where she worked, she told me she was really pleased and proud of me. By this time she was working in a women's clothes shop, as Dixon's had been burned down by IRA firebombs in 1975. She said she'd be on her lunch break in half an hour and to come back to see her then. I wandered up to Woolworth's where my sister worked on a Saturday and then returned to my mum. She took me out for lunch to the Wimpy as a treat.

"Don't tell Joanna though," she said. "I don't want to upset her."

We ordered sausage and chips. While we were waiting, my mum said, "Make sure you make the most of the High School. I never had the chance like you. You know, I passed. Even won a scholarship. And there were only four given out in the whole of Belfast. I could have gone to grammar school, could have made something of myself, but I never got the opportunity. Now you've got the chance. Don't waste it."

"Why didn't you go?"

"There just wasn't the money."

"But what about the scholarship? I thought if you won a scholarship, that meant everything was paid for you."

"Well, that's not what your granda thought. He was worried about uniforms and gymslips and books. And our Ruth was already ill, so there wasn't the money spare."

"Oh, I'm so sorry, Mummy. You must have been heartbroken over it."

"Oh, I was heartbroken all right, but not over the scholarship. I didn't even know about that until six years ago when Simon passed his eleven-plus. Your granda told me when I was up visiting them one day on my own. I was telling them about Simon passing and how proud I was, and he said, "Sure he takes after you. Didn't you win a scholarship when you were eleven?" And he opened up that cupboard above his chair, rooted in the back and took out an old yellowing letter, still in its envelope. It was from the Belfast examining board offering me a scholarship. He'd never shown it to anyone since he received it in 1944 until that day in 1971. Even your granny knew nothing about it. So it wasn't the scholarship that broke my heart. He never even told me I'd passed. I went around for years thinking I'd failed."

I felt really bad for my mother. I wondered what my granny thought about my granda's decision.

"You know my mummy won a scholarship?" I said to her. "Well, why did Granda not let her take it?"

"There's things you can't understand at your age," she said. "This is one of them."

"But would you have agreed with him, if he'd've told you about it at the time?"

"That's between me and your granda."

I let it drop. "Shall I put the TV on for the parade?" I said.

We watched the coverage for a couple of hours, as thousands of Orangemen, accompanied by an array of loyalist bands—flute, accordion, brass, even pipe—marched through the city centre to the field. We caught the merest glimpse of my granda as he came through on the far side of the camera. And I spotted Johnny and Pete, Janice, who played in a girls' accordion band, and my Uncle George.

George's lodge was preceded by a woman in her seventies, decked out in a Union Jack outfit and wearing a wide-brimmed hat adorned with orange lilies, the loyalist flower. "And here's Orange Lily," the commentator said. "She's looking in fine form this year."

At midday I asked my granny if she wanted me to put anything on for our dinner.

"Are you hungry?" she asked.

"Not very," I answered, "but if we don't put something on now, we'll not get dinner at 12.30."

"Ah, never worry about that. That's just your granda. We'll eat when it suits us. I got us one of them Fray Bentos steak and kidney pies from the shop yesterday, as a treat. We just need to stick it in the oven when we're ready."

"Oh, I love those. I'll make some mash to go with it if you like. Or chips. Which would you prefer?"

We decided on mash, but it was another hour before I switched off the TV and started peeling the potatoes and sticking the pie in the oven. My granny had also bought me a bottle of Club Orange, my favourite fizzy drink. It felt like a real feast, eating off trays on our laps in the living room, instead of round the table in the pantry.

When we'd finished eating, I said, "Oh, Granny, that was fantastic. What more could you want than Fray Bentos, mash and Club Orange?"

She laughed.

"Go and have a look in the freezer box," she said.

I went into the pantry where they kept their small fridge. Inside the tiny freezer compartment was a slab of Walls Neapolitan ice cream. I shrieked in delight.

"Oh, Granny, you've got all my favourite things. How did you know about the Neapolitan ice cream?"

"I'm not your granny for nothing," was her reply. "There's wafers, Flakes and raspberry ripple sauce in the cupboard."

I couldn't believe how much thought she'd put into getting things I'd like. I went and hugged her.

"Thanks, Granny. Thanks a lot."

She smiled. "Go and get your ice cream."

"Are you not having any?" I said.

"No, thanks, love, it's not my thing. But put the kettle on. There's a bar of Fry's Peppermint Cream in the drawer that I've been saving, and I just fancy it now with a cup of tea."

While we were eating our puddings, she said, "Now, what do you want to do for the rest of the day? Your granda's lodge won't be back before six."

"I don't know," I said. "What do you want to do?"

"Nothing too energetic. I'm not up to it these days. Shall we see what's on the TV?"

I switched on the TV and we contemplated our limited viewing options: a film that had already started, horse racing or a repeat of *Horizon*. We settled on the film but it held our attention for only five minutes before we drifted back to talking. I rarely got the chance to talk on my own to my granny and we covered all sorts: from our favourite sandwich fillings—chips for me, cooked ham for my granny; to life after death—both hoping for heaven, me fearing hell; to why she preferred stockings to tights—couldn't be doing with the gusset; to how she came to marry my granda.

She'd been born in 1904 into a working-class family in the staunchly loyalist Shankill area of west Belfast, the sixth of ten children, three of whom died in infancy. Her parents adored each other.

"They were known as the Darby and Joan of the Shankill," she said.

"Who were Darby and Joan?" I asked.

"Well, I'm not sure I know myself," she said, but it means a couple that is always together."

Her father was a barber. Her mother managed the money well to keep the family fed, but they never had much. At twelve, my granny started work in one of Belfast's linen mills. It was long and hard work, but she stuck it out for seven years. Then, when she was twenty, she got the chance of a job at Gallaher's cigarette factory. It was there that she met my granda.

"Oh, he was a good-looking man, your granda. I thought that the first day I saw him in the canteen."

She opened up the cupboard above my granda's rocking chair and riffled through the photograph albums before extracting a very old blue one, which she brought over to the sofa.

I opened it gently. The first picture was a sepia-tinted one of my granny looking very glamorous in a short, straight, dark bob and a long-waisted dress.

"When was this, Granny?"

"That was taken on my twenty-first birthday, February 1925."

The next two were black and white photos of my granda as a young man. In the first he was leaning against a wall, jet-black hair swept away from his face, a smile twitching at the corner of his mouth. He was handsome—a cross between James Stewart and Cary Grant. No wonder he'd caught my granny's eye. In the second he was wearing a flat black cap and standing next to another, slightly shorter, young man.

"Who's that?"

"Some man that worked with yer granda. McLuskey, I think his name was. Died of consumption."

The next picture was of my grandparents together, him standing with his arm protectively around her shoulders.

"That's only a few months after we were married. I'd just discovered I was pregnant, had told him the day before. He was proud as punch."

"Was that Ruth you were having?"

"Aye, it was." She was quiet for a moment, then turned the page to two pictures of a chubby toddler on her own, smiling straight to camera in the first photo, sitting on my granny's lap in the second. I was careful not to ask any more questions. My granny was still sensitive on the subject of Ruth, even twenty-five years after her death.

The next photo was of a baby, bonny in spite of being almost bald, dressed in a white robe and booties, lying on her back on a sofa. On the opposite page, a girl scowled out from the other end of the sofa.

"That's your mummy," my granny said, pointing to the first photo, "and that's her with Ruth."

"She doesn't look very happy, does she, Granny?"

My granny let out a little laugh.

"Furious she was when your mother was born. For about the first year. She'd wanted a brother. I suppose we all had."

We turned the next page: a few years later and my mother about four, her sister's arm around her shoulders, both smiling.

"Oh, you're the spit of her," my granny said.

Except that it was black and white, the picture of my mother as a child was just like an image of me in our album at home.

"Since the day and hour I saw you, I've always said, 'That's Maisie's child.' It used to really annoy your father. Mind you, none of you take for him. Except for Simon's green eyes, you've not a feature between you that comes from his side." She nodded with some satisfaction.

"But what about our Joanna?" I said. "Simon and I look like Mummy, but Joanna doesn't."

"Aye, she might not look like your mummy, I'll give you that. But does she look like your daddy, or Granny McCullagh, or Gertrude?"

I pulled their images up in my mind, considering.

"No, she's not like any of them either. So who does she take after?"

"Well, I'm not saying it's the complete picture, but look at this." She flicked on a few pages to a photo of Ruth and put her hand over the lower face, leaving only the nose upwards. "What do you think?"

"Oh, you're right, Granny. The eyes and forehead are just like our Joanna. I've never noticed that before. What about the rest of her face?"

"Well, that I've never quite worked out myself, though I've puzzled over it. Maybe Maggie, your granda's sister. I don't know. But one thing's for sure, it's definitely not your da."

With a sense of triumph she settled back on the sofa and let out a sigh of pleasure.

"What age was Ruth when this one was taken?" I asked.

"About fourteen. Your mother would have been eight. It was the last summer before Ruth got ill." She paused. "Rheumatic fever. Sleeping on damp blankets in the air-raid shelter. I'm sure that's what caused it. It left her with a weakened heart. She was never the same." She paused again.

"You asked earlier about why your granda didn't let your mother take her scholarship. Well, he did it for the best as he saw it. By then we were nearly three years into Ruth's illness. It wasn't like it is now. There was no NHS then. We had to pay for every treatment, every drop of medicine. There just wasn't the money. And anyway, what would have been the point? Girls didn't need an education then, especially not girls from round here. I didn't work after I was married, and your granda expected it would be the same for your mummy. Things are different now. I know it must seem strange to you, but he did his best, and there's an end to it. And sure, didn't it work out all right for her? Sure she's got three of the loveliest children in the world."

She made no mention of the man who'd fathered them.

"But she might've been happier if she'd had the chance of an education. And she could still have had us as well. That's what I'm going to do, Granny. A career and children."

"Knowing you, you will, too," she said. Then, "What makes you think your mummy's not happy?"

I couldn't say, "Because she sits in the house in the

evening and tells me that she wishes she was dead," or that
when we were walking on the beach a few weeks ago she said,
"One of these days I'll turn out to sea and just keep walking."
So I said, "Oh I don't know. Just sometimes she says she wishes she'd had the chance to be a social worker instead of working in a clothes shop."

"People will always need clothes," my granny replied.

I had no answer to that, so I made a cup of tea. Soon it
was time to go and meet the men returning from the field.
My granny came down to the bottom of the street and we
clapped the lodge home.

Chapter 18

The Wasteground

MY GRANDA'S FEET were sore the next day from the march, though he still forced himself to the paper shop at six o'clock. But he wanted a restful day at home. We sat reading the papers after breakfast and then played cards. Although I was getting better at poker, I was still no match for my granda, and I was down to my last two burnt matches when there was a knock at the door around ten o'clock. It was Janice.

"How's your feet?" my granda asked.

"Not too bad, Mr Linton. And your own?"

"Aye, the same," he said, flashing a warning glance at me. "Was that your first full march, Janice?"

"It was, Mr Linton. It's some distance all the same, isn't it? I was worn out last night. Fell asleep in front of the telly as soon as I'd had my tea."

"Aye, it is tiring right enough," my granda said. "You'll want to take it easy today."

"Well, actually I came down to see if Constance wanted to go to the playground."

"The playground? I'd've thought you'd be a bit tired for the playground. Do you not fancy a wee game of cards instead?"

We played cards for the rest of the morning, poker till my

granda had won all our matchsticks, then gin rummy and pontoon. Janice went home to let us have our dinner at half twelve, but I arranged to call for her an hour later to go to the playground.

When I got there she said, "Let's not go to the playground. I've had a better idea. Let's go to the wasteground and look for treasure."

The wasteground was a nearby patch of derelict land reached by the steps up from Crosscollyer Street to the Limestone Road. It was the size of a couple of football pitches and was covered with a combination of building rubble, weeds, fragments of unidentifiable machinery and abandoned household objects.

On our way, we bumped into Pete and Johnny, who decided to come with us. We scrubbed around for a while but only found a large rusted metal spring, a TV aerial and assorted bits of broken pottery. We gave up and instead started chucking stones at a nearby oil can, cheering if someone hit it.

Tiring of this too, we all went to sit on a flattish bit of ground away from the road. The others talked of being on the march the day before. It was the first full march for Pete and Janice, the second for Johnny. There were stories of stones being thrown from Catholic areas, of people with blisters the size of their feet, of someone in the boys' band throwing up after taking a load of drink at the field. I laughed at their stories, egging them on to grander and grander exaggerations.

I wondered afterwards if that had been my error. One minute we were talking about how high Johnny could throw his baton and how loudly Pete could play his flute, and the next Johnny had grabbed me from behind, his knees pinning my shoulders to the ground, his arms holding mine hard, while Pete pressed on top of me, one hand clamped over my mouth, the other trying to unzip my trousers.

I'm still not clear how it happened, how Johnny got behind me so quickly without me realising what he was going to do, how Pete got on top without me managing to kick out.

I felt his hand release the top button of my jeans, then pull down my zip. And then he was struggling with his own trousers. He arched his back, lifting his head up so he could focus on undoing his flies. His hand came away from my mouth and quickly released his button and zip. In a moment his penis burst free.

"No, Pete. Please, no. Don't do this. No."

He looked into my eyes for the first time. Just a glance, then away to Johnny.

"Go on," said Johnny. "Go on. Do it."

Pete looked at me again.

"Please don't," I said.

He let out a deep breath, then rolled off me. Johnny too released his grip. I got to my feet, sobbing, and started half running, half hobbling off across the wasteground, pulling my jeans back up and fastening them. Janice sat where she had been throughout the whole event. She didn't come with me, but the boys didn't follow either. Somehow I knew they wouldn't.

I stopped running when I got to the steps at the top of Crosscollyer Street. I knew I looked a state. I started taking deep breaths and forcing calm into my body. I walked slowly down the steps and carried on along Mountcollyer Avenue. I turned left at the bottom and made my way to the playground. I stopped at the water fountain and washed my face and hands. I combed my hair with my fingers, removing bits of grit from the wasteground. Then I walked back to my grandparents' house. It was almost time for tea anyway, and they noticed nothing out of the ordinary.

"Did you have a good time?" my granny asked.

"Yes, thanks," I heard myself answering. "Is there anything I can do to help with the tea?"

"No, you're all right. It'll be ready soon."

We followed our usual routine for the rest of the evening. In bed that night I examined the bruises that had come up on my arms and legs. I'd have to be careful to keep them covered.

The next day it was pouring with rain. It gave me a good excuse for staying in. I played cards, read and chatted with my grandparents as if everything was normal, hoping that Janice wouldn't come round. I didn't want to see her again, didn't want her round telling my grandparents what had happened. What would they think of me if they found out? Maybe I *was* bad.

On Friday I went with my granda on the weekly visit to the Grove Public Baths, the scene of my first encounter with Janice only a week earlier. He went to the slipper baths as usual, so I didn't need to worry about him seeing my bruises. The trip passed off without incident, and by midday I was back in the safety of my grandparents' house, helping my granny peel the potatoes for our chips.

The rain came on again in the afternoon, so I didn't need a reason for avoiding the playground. My granda wondered why Janice hadn't popped in for a game of cards but didn't suggest I go and fetch her. I went to bed that night relieved that I'd only one more day to get through before I could escape back to Coleraine. The rain cleared overnight, and I woke the next day to a bright sunny Belfast morning.

"So, what are your plans for your last day?" my granda asked over breakfast. "I suppose you'll want to see Janice and them ones you've met while you've been here."

"I'd rather have the time with you and my granny," I answered truthfully.

"Have you fallen out with her?" he asked, suspicious.

"No, Granda. Maybe I'll catch her later in the playground. But I wanted to go with you to the park and maybe my Aunt Edie's this morning, and then maybe I could do something with my granny this afternoon."

"Aye, well, it's a better day, so a walk to the park would be nice right enough," he said.

We set off about ten, after the papers and a quick game or two of cards. It was good to be out and about, but the walk past the playground was a tense moment. We fed the ducks and then went to watch the bowls. I'd been to bowls before. It had been one of my father's fads, though his interest waned after losing the play-off for the Christmas turkey to Mr Hamilton from the wool shop. Mind you, it was no disgrace losing to Mr Hamilton, who made it into the Great Britain team for the Montreal Olympics the following year.

My granda and I sat mostly in companionable silence, making the most of the Saturday-morning sunshine, exchanging the odd comment on the performances on the green. At midday he said, "We'd best be getting back for dinner. We'll have to leave your Aunt Edie till later."

I took my time washing up the plates after we'd eaten—I was still three and a half hours from the safety of teatime.

When I'd finished clearing up, I suggested a game of cards, but for once my granda declined.

"I thought you wanted to go up to see your Aunt Edie."

"I do. Were you thinking of going now?"

"Shortly. I think your granny's going to take a walk out with us as well."

The ten-minute walk felt like two hours. I wanted to hurry, but my granny wasn't up to it. We plodded along, my heart pounding at every footstep, every slamming door. I kept my eyes away when we passed the wasteground on the Limestone Road. Edie finished work at lunchtime on a Saturday. She was installed at home in her housecoat and slippers, smoking a cigarette, when we arrived at her door. My granda gave her the cigarettes that he got from Gallaher's every month.

"Ah, Uncle Michael, Aunt Peggy. Great to see you. Come on in. And you, Constance," she said. "Do you fancy a cup of tea?"

"I'll make it," I offered.

"Ah, you're a good girl," she said.

I filled the kettle and lit the main ring on the stove. While it was boiling, I scooped some Punjana tea into the pot.

"Constance," I heard my aunt call from the front room. "There's some custard tarts in the fridge and some jam ones in the cupboard. Throw some of them on a plate, will you?"

By the time I got the tarts out, the kettle was boiled. I scalded the tea leaves, swirled the pot a few times, then filled it up and put it on the stove to draw. I took the tarts through first, then mugs of hot, strong tea.

"Ah, you make a great cup of tea," Aunt Edie said. I settled down in the front room on the sofa next to my aunt. "God, you get more and more like your mother every day," she said to me. Then, turning to my grandparents, "Isn't she the spit of Maisie? It'll not be long before you're turning some fella's head," she said, bursting into a wheezy laugh that ended in a cough as I reddened and looked at the carpet.

"Your mother could have had her pick of suitors. Oh, I had some times with her at the dances. We used to have to run like the clappers to get home on time for you, Uncle Michael."

She started into stories of her youth. My granda joined in with tales of his teens, and then they both got on to the blitz in Belfast. They were both great storytellers and kept granny and me amused. It was just after four when we left. My last danger run. We didn't have to pass the playground, though I could hear the shouts as we approached the end of Mountcollyer Road. We turned left. Only two hundred yards to go. One hundred yards, fifty, home. I'd made it.

Chapter 19

An Affair to Remember

"THANK GOD YOU'RE coming home," my sister said in a hushed voice.

We were out in the yard at my grandparents' on the Sunday that they'd come to pick me up. I had stayed home with my granny to wait for them while my granda went off to church.

They were due at half eleven, but it was twenty past twelve before they arrived. I could feel the tension between them but for more than an hour hadn't had the chance to find out what was going on.

First my granda had arrived home from church, then we'd had Sunday dinner, and finally we'd settled down in the front room.

"Oh, I'm feeling a bit hot in here," I said. "I think I'll go out and get some air in the yard."

I signalled to Joanna with my eyes for her to follow.

"Yes, it's a bit stuffy," she said. "I think I'll get some air as well."

Before I had the chance to ask her anything, she was already in with her "Thank God you're coming home".

"Why, what's been happening?" I said.

She rolled her eyes. "You've no idea. It's been hell. Pure hell. I am in so much trouble."

"What's been going on?"

"I'm not supposed to talk about it."

"Who says?"

"Both of them. Both of them said I was never to mention it again."

"Mention what?"

"That Daddy's been having an affair. Or at least I thought he'd been having an affair. Sandra Milligan told me. You know that she was doing work experience at his office. Said she found out while she was there that he was having an affair. So I went and told Mummy. Told her she should keep her eye out."

"So did she?"

"No, she just went and told him that *I'd said* he was having an affair. You've no idea what it was like. He went mental. Said I was shit stirring. Trying to cause trouble. Said I was being malicious. Said that Sandra was a half-wit and that anyone who believed what she said was a bloody fool.

"So then they both had a go at me over tea. Why had I said it? Why did I believe it? Why didn't I realise that he'd never do anything like that? Went on and on as if he'd never done it before."

It took a moment for her words to sink in. "Hold on. What do you mean, done it before?"

"He's done it before. Don't you remember Vivienne?"

"Vivienne? Vivienne who?"

"Vivienne. That woman he took us to meet."

"When? When did he take us? I don't remember."

"Och, Constance. You must remember Vivienne. She was quite tall. Dark haired. Grey eyes. He took us a few times. On a Saturday, when Mummy was first working."

Slowly, through fog, it came back to me. Driving down to Portrush. Stopping just outside to pick up a woman waiting at the bus stop. Driving on to the car park near the west strand where he'd drop me and Joanna off to play on the swings or walk on the beach.

"I won't be long, girls," he'd say, as he drove off with her.

Sometimes it would be thirty minutes, sometimes an hour, once an hour and a half, but eventually he'd come back on his own.

"Come on now," he'd say. "We'll go shopping. Here's some extra pocket money."

How could I have forgotten something so important?

"So what happened about Vivienne?" I asked Joanna. "Did we tell Mummy about her?"

"Oh, no. He told us not to mention her, so we didn't. But she found out anyway."

"How?"

"I don't know. Someone told her, but I don't know who."

"So why didn't she leave him?" I asked.

"I don't know."

"So is it true? Has he done it again?"

"He says he hasn't, and she believes him."

"Do you believe him?"

She hesitated.

"They think so. That's all that matters. That's what keeps them off my back."

I nodded. We started at the sound of the back door opening. It was my granny.

"Your Uncle George is here," she said.

"We'll be just in," Joanna replied. She turned back to me.

"You mustn't let on you know. Not give him any hint. You know I'd be for it."

"I know. I won't."

"Thanks." She squeezed my hand briefly. Then we went back inside.

Chapter 20

Split Lip

THE NEWS OF my father's affair was unsettling. But a few weeks later something happened that shook my foundations further. The Queen was visiting the university at Coleraine in August as part of her Silver Jubilee celebrations. We lived on the other side of the river from the university, and the army was crawling all over the area.

The day before the visit, Clare and I chatted with a group of Brits outside my front gate.

"What are you looking for?" Clare said.

"Anyfink dodgy," one of the soldiers said, in a strange English accent.

"But why are you looking here?" I asked. "We're not even that close to the university."

"Not by road," he said. "But you are as the crow flies. Here, have a look through my gunsight."

He stood behind me, still holding the gun, as I positioned myself between his arms. Through the sight we were almost by the river. He panned to the left, and the edge of the university zoomed into sight.

"Wow!" I said.

"Can I have a go?" Clare said. We swapped positions.

"But still, I don't see why you're outside my house. Look at the flag." A Red Hand of Ulster flag with a Union Jack in the top left-hand corner was hanging in the garden for marching season. "We're Protestants. We're not a danger. It's the Catholics you have to worry about."

His answer shocked me.

"I'm a Catholic." He laughed as I struggled for words. "Anyway, we're pulling out now. See ya."

"Did you know they had Catholics in the army?" I asked Clare.

She shrugged. "Shall we go out on the bikes?" she said.

I agreed, but as I cycled along I kept thinking about the soldier. How could the problem be Catholics if there were Catholics in the army? Nothing made sense.

The following month, September 1977, Clare and I started at Coleraine High School. We walked to school together on our first morning, along with my back-door neighbour Katy Bradley and her older sister Margaret.

I was excited and nervous as I hopped over Katy's fence in my bottle-green uniform. It was second-hand, bought from the Craigs who were moving away from Coleraine. I'd have preferred a new uniform, but it didn't look too bad. I'd managed to remove the Laura Craig name tags with careful use of a razor blade.

I walked up the Bradleys' garden path and skirted round the house. Katy was standing at the front door having her photograph taken. I waited with an impatient Margaret by the gate.

"Honestly, you'd think no one had ever started the High School before. I suppose you've been through this performance as well."

I found a plausible lie. "Oh, I think they've decided to wait until I get my tie."

Like other beginners, I sported naked shirt buttons that first day. I wouldn't have a tie until I was allocated to my house. There were four houses, Cranagh, Culrath, Fermoyle and Inverbann, each with a different coloured tie. I liked the deep purple of Inverbann best, but my mum was hoping for the yellowish gold of Fermoyle—Mrs Craig had thrown in Laura's old Fermoyle tie as part of the package.

The walk to school took about twenty minutes, and by half past eight we were walking into the big red-brick building of the main school block. Margaret led us to the first-year cloakrooms, then left us to the task of finding our own hooks. They were organised alphabetically by form. I left Clare searching among 1B while I went to find my own name in 1A.

The bell went at ten to nine. I followed the crowd through to the hall, lining up, as directed by a prefect, in the front row. I looked down the line. There were only a few faces that I recognised from the Christie—Jacqueline Henderson, Laverne Boyd, Fiona McMillan—but none that I'd been friendly with. After assembly, our prefect took us to our form room, on the third floor of the old building. We'd been asked to bring a book in to read on the first day. I'd agonised about it the night before. We didn't have many books in the house—some Enid Blytons I'd accumulated over years of birthdays and Christmases, my Christie memorial prizes, the odd thriller of my mum's. None of them felt suitable. But then I found *Love for Lydia* outside my brother's room. His girlfriend, Lorna, had left it behind. I decided to borrow it. It was as good a choice as that of anyone else in the class.

I walked home with Clare. We'd sworn to stay best friends, but even after a day I knew this was unlikely. Each of us would have to find a new allegiance within our own form. But that day we were still pretending it was all as it had been, and so we arranged to go to the swimming pool together on the Saturday afternoon.

I called round for her after lunch, but we took our time getting to the pool, meandering through town, calling in at favourite haunts in order that our food had time to go down before the swim. It was a quarter to three before we paid our money over for a double session. I always hoped for a private cubicle in the changing rooms, but as usual was stuck with undressing in the public area. At least I'd already put my costume on beneath my clothes. Soon we were in the pool, doing underwater handstands and somersaults, racing each other and practising our diving.

We'd been there about half an hour when disaster struck. One minute I was standing in the shallow end, contemplating another underwater trick. The next, my lip was splitting apart, blood pumping into the pool. A young man had decided to start the backstroke without checking to see who or what was behind him, and in my focus on what new gymnastic feat I might try, I hadn't noticed him. He'd gathered himself into the wall and then thrust back with great force.

It was his head that did me the damage. The back of his skull connected with my upper lip, and the pressure between his bone and my teeth split my lip right apart. I didn't feel the pain so much as the force in the first instant as he knocked me off balance. But as the pool reddened around me and I began to take in the horror on Clare's face, it suddenly zoomed in. "Ow! Ow!" My hand went to my mouth and came away bright red. I staggered towards the steps and began to pull myself up them, one-handed. The other hand stayed at my bleeding mouth.

As I blundered out of the pool, a lifeguard appeared beside me, rather in the manner of the shopkeeper from *Mr Benn*. It was Jimmy, an older man in a tracksuit who I'd always kept away from.

"Come on. Over here," he said. "Come on. You're all right."

I let him lead me to one of the benches that were fixed around all four sides of the pool. Instinctively my tongue assessed the damage. I tried to make sense of the gap I could feel, but the pain was really beginning to take a grip now. And the blood. The overwhelming taste of blood in my mouth. There was so much blood.

Jimmy passed me a huge wad of tissue to staunch the flow.

"Are you with anyone?" he asked.

I looked around for Clare. She was standing nearby. I gestured in her direction.

"Any adults?"

I shook my head.

"Are either of your parents at home?"

I nodded.

"OK. That's good. Well, it's not bleeding so badly now, but from the look of it, you'll have to be stitched. Go and get changed and then phone home."

He handed me some more tissue and then returned to his usual station. I sat dabbing gently at my bloody lip. Maybe it would be OK, I told myself. Maybe it would stop bleeding soon. Maybe I wouldn't have to go to hospital. Much more than having my lip stitched back together, I dreaded having to call my father.

I'd had to call him once before, years earlier, after spraining my ankle. I'd fallen over a tree root on a Brownie treasure hunt in the grounds of the manor house on the other side of Coleraine. I thought I'd be able to limp home, but Brown Owl insisted that I call my father to come and collect me. She helped me up to the big house and stood nearby as I dialled the number. He went up the wall, shouting down the phone about what kind of a bloody useless great lump I was. I'm sure Brown Owl heard every word, but luckily she didn't say anything. Even so, I never went back to Brownies after that.

Clare came and sat down beside me.

"Oohh, it looks terrible. It must be sore," she said.

"Is." I answered as best as I could, but my lips were out of my control. We sat for a moment.

"Shall we go and get changed?" she asked.

Clare put her arm round me and we walked together to the changing rooms. We were in the middle of a session and the place was fairly empty. For once I got a cubicle.

I dressed slowly, blood still splashing around my feet— costume off first, drying with my towel, then knickers and jeans. Sitting down to dry my feet, then socks and shoes. I took a deep breath—time to start on my top half.

I'd been wearing a bra for only a week and still struggled with doing the catch up. I decided not to bother. I looked at my T-shirt. It was one of my favourites, white with the silhouette of a skateboarder on the front. I stretched the neck as wide as I could and pulled it over my head. I yelped in pain as it slipped past my mouth.

"Are you OK?" Clare asked from the next cubicle.

"Mmmm," I answered through the tissue that was back to my bleeding lip. With my other hand I fumbled my costume and towel into my duffle bag. It was time to face the mirror.

I'd hoped that somehow it wouldn't be too bad, that I

wouldn't need to go to hospital. The mirror shattered such hopes. The great black clots congealed around my mouth were bad enough, but it was the state of my top lip that was most disturbing. The lip had split right open, one half folded over the other. There was nothing for it. I dug a 2p out of my pocket and made my way to the public phone in the reception.

Clare leaned against the opposite wall, trying to keep out of earshot, but ready if I beckoned her over. I picked up the receiver and dialled the number—3 . . . 8 . . . 7 . . . 4. I heard it ringing. Once, twice, three times. He answered on the sixth ring, the pips drowning him out. I forced the money into the machine in a panic.

"McCullagh speaking."

"Hetho," I said thickly, finding speech a challenge. "Dath. It's Constance."

"What the hell are you phoning for? You know what time it is."

Of course I knew what time it was: 3.55 p.m. It was part of why I hadn't wanted to phone. If my dad was at home on a Saturday afternoon, he would invariably be watching the wrestling.

"Thorry."

"I'm missing the wrestling. Hurry up. What do you want?"

"I've hath an accident. At the pool. They said you need to come and take me to hospital."

"Oh, Jesus Christ. What the fuck have you done now? You're fucking useless."

"Thorry."

"And it's Mick McManus today."

"Thorry."

"This is the last time."

He put the phone down. Slowly I returned the receiver.

"Is he coming?" Clare asked.

I nodded.

"Do you want me to wait with you?"

I shook my head. "Be OK. Thanks."

I watched as she swung her bag over her shoulder and set off for home.

Then I settled down opposite the main door to wait.

Chapter 21

Drinking for Victory

I T HAD BEEN drummed into me from an early age not to swim immediately after eating or who knew what might befall you.

"You've got to let your food go down," my mum would say.

"But it is down."

"Not far enough. It needs time to settle. You must wait at least an hour after eating. It's just too big a risk."

But no one had ever mentioned drinking. No one had ever said, "You must wait at least one hour after drinking the vodka you filched from your dad's drinks cabinet before swimming."

It was March 1979 and I was at the local pool, scene of my split lip, for the Coleraine and District inter-schools swimming gala. The night before, instead of thinking how I was going to win the breaststroke, I was wondering whether I could get away with stealing some vodka from my father's drinks cabinet and smuggling it into the gala in my blue tupperware beaker.

It wasn't the first time I'd nicked drink from him. The previous month I'd had a go at his gin. He'd been away on a business trip at the time. My brother was at university, and both my sister and mother were out, Joanna at a disco, Mum at a church social. So I was in the house on my own on a Friday evening, bored. I decided I'd have a little snowball to cheer myself up. I'd had a sip of one at Christmas and I'd rather liked it.

Even though no one was due home for hours, I sneaked into the lounge, straining for the least hint of someone returning. I opened up the drinks cabinet and took out the Advocaat. I poured an inch into a glass and added a dash of lime cordial. Then I carefully returned the two bottles to the cabinet.

I slipped out of the lounge and into the kitchen. We'd no white lemonade, but there was a little bit of brown and a full bottle of pineappleade in the larder. I filled my glass up with the remains of the brown lemonade and took it through to the living room with some digestive biscuits spread with butter. I settled down in front of the telly to enjoy my drink.

When it was finished I decided to have another, but as the lemonade had run out I went for gin and pineappleade. It was foul. The smell of the gin reminded me of nothing as much as the Vosene shampoo my father used, and even the pineappleade didn't mask its taste. But I soldiered on with it, welcoming the blurring edges.

It had been a difficult couple of months. Christmas was always a bit tense in our family. Then, at the beginning of January, my Granny Linton died suddenly. It was a Sunday morning and we were getting ready for church when the phone rang. I was in the hallway brushing my hair and picked up the receiver.

"Could you get your mummy?" my granda said. His voice sounded shaky and faint. My grandparents didn't have a telephone, and I'd known him phone only once before, one August evening a couple of years earlier. We'd been out at the Oul' Lammas fair in Ballycastle. The phone was ringing as we arrived home. My mum dashed to answer it. It was my granda to tell her that my granny had suffered a mild stroke.

I knew it must be something bad. I sprinted upstairs to tell my mum that Granda was on the phone. She picked up the extension in her bedroom. I hovered by the door.

"Oh, no," she said. "Please God, no." She sat down on the bed. "Oh, Daddy."

She didn't say anything for a minute. Then, "I'm so sorry, Daddy. I'll get there as soon as I can."

My father emerged from the bathroom just as my mum came off the phone. She was just sitting on the bed staring straight ahead.

"Maisie, are you all right?" Still she sat staring.

"I think something serious has happened," I said. "Granda phoned."

"Maisie, is it your mum? Is she OK?"

"She's dead," my mum said, and suddenly she started to sob.

My mum got the train to Belfast later that day. She was away for the next few days. We stayed at home with my father until the funeral. It was the first funeral I'd been to. My mum took me upstairs to see my granny laid out in the front room. I hung back near the door.

"Come over and see her," she said. "You don't need to be scared. She looks just like herself." My mum took me by the hand. I walked with her over to the coffin. My granny looked so small in the coffin. So small. But very peaceful.

"You should touch her," my mum said. "It'll help you accept she's gone."

She kissed my granny on the forehead. I did the same. Then I started to cry and so did my mum. Downstairs my granda was sitting by the fire, tears dribbling down his face. He made no effort to wipe them away. I'd never seen my granda cry. I didn't know how to manage it. I looked away, embarrassed. The minister conducted the service in my grandparents' packed house. Afterwards the coffin was carried down the street, and then into the hearse and off to the city cemetery.

My mum came home with us the next day, but she was only half alive. She was like that for weeks, until she and my dad had a fight one night. He was going away to Dublin for the weekend and was panicking because he'd come down with piles.

"What am I going to do, Maisie?"

"The doctor's given you cream. Just follow his instructions. I'm sure you'll be fine."

"But what if I'm not? What if they start bleeding? How will I manage?"

"Victor, you'll just have to manage. I'm past caring what you do with your piles."

I'd never heard her talk to him like this before. Neither had he. He lifted up a saucepan. I saw it flying through the air. It caught her on the side of the head. I saw her hand go to her face, but I couldn't hear any sound any more. My father stormed out of the kitchen. He slammed the door, but I couldn't hear it. And then he left the house.

I think the second gin was a mistake. It was a generous measure, and I topped the bottle up carefully with water.

oping that the green glass would prevent close inspection. By halfway through the second, I was aware of feeling a little bit queasy, but I carried on. Waste not, want not.

But the third—that was definitely going too far.

My mother was surprised when she came home and found me in my room—normally you had to beat me to bed. But I just said I wasn't feeling well, which was true. I felt even worse the next day—my first hangover—but dragged myself to school for our hockey match against Ballymena Academy. I was team captain, and as long as I could stand, I'd play. Miss Park thought I was a hero for turning up when I wasn't well, but I was definitely not on my game. And my poor performance seemed to percolate throughout the team. By half-time we were 2-0 down.

"Come on, girls," Miss Park said. "Where's the fight? Where's the determination? I need something more than I'm getting from you. I've never seen you play so badly. Constance, I know you're not well, but what's wrong with the rest of you?"

"It's your own fault you're not well, drinking yourself silly," Julie Morton, the left inner, muttered to me.

I looked down and said nothing. Miss Park wasn't so quiet.

"What did you just say?" she said to Julie.

"Nothing," Julie said.

She, too, was looking down by now.

"Don't nothing me. What did you say?"

"I said, it's her own fault she's not well when she was drinking herself silly last night."

Miss Park was usually very easygoing, but I could feel her switch.

"Girls, go and practise some passing. Constance, I want word." The others jogged off. "Were you drinking last night

I didn't speak.

"Answer me. Is it true?"

I nodded.

"You have no idea how angry I am with you. What wer you thinking? Drinking at thirteen? I can't believe it. I don know what I'm going to do about this, but one thing's ce tain, Constance, you'd better make sure we win. Becaus you've no idea how much trouble you'll be in with me if yo don't."

I scored a hat trick in the second half. We won 3-2.

She had a serious talk with me the following Monda about the dangers of alcohol and not growing up too young but that was it. I listened and nodded, but there was no way was giving up already.

My mother was in the night before the swimming gal but she never suspected me of anything. I slipped into th lounge with my beaker and opened up the drinks cabine There were four bottles of spirits to choose from. Even th thought of the gin made me want to gag. The same went fo the whiskey; I'd been force fed it hot for a cold since I wa young and could not abide the smell, let alone the taste of it That left vodka or poteen.

The poteen was passing itself off as tonic water. My dac had bought it from a farmer from Ballymena. I was scared o the poteen. I'd heard stories of it sending people blind, and I'd seen for myself what it had done to my brother and his best friend at New Year, Simon lying sprawled in the from porch while Fenton threw everyone—including me—out o our house. I had to wait next door in my neighbours' house till my parents came home from the rugby club dinner dance. Simon stopped drinking for three weeks afterwards and swore he'd never go near poteen again.

I don't know why my dad even bought it in the first place. Although he liked the occasional drop of alcohol, he wasn't a big drinker. Not like his father. Granda McCullagh could really put the drink away.

"He'd have drunk it from a shitty glass," my mother pronounced, out of my father's hearing.

He died when my dad was ten, of a combination of consumption and drink. My mother said there were wreaths from every pub in the area, and in Belfast that's a lot of wreaths.

I opted for the vodka. As before, I replaced what I'd taken with water and hoped for the best. I went to bed feeling pleased with myself.

The next morning I set off with my swimming costume, cap and towel in one bag and my packed lunch in the other. The gala started at half past nine with the heats for my event, under-13 girls' 25-metre breaststroke, scheduled for a quarter past ten. I sat with my team-mates shouting on the High School competitors.

As the time for my race approached, I slipped out of my tracksuit top and pulled on my swimming cap ready for my race. There were four heats in my event, with the winners qualifying for the final along with the two fastest losers.

Joanna McAleese, also from the High School, won the first heat. I watched as she clambered out of the pool and rejoined the rest of the High School team. I didn't know the girl who won the next heat. The third heat was won by Mary Anne McCabe from Loreto Covent. I recognised her from hockey. We'd played an ill-tempered match against them the previous month. I hoped I'd get the chance to beat her later that day. At last it was my heat. I was called forward along with the other five in my race.

"Take your marks."

I got into position and focused my mind.

"Get set."

Win, win, win.

"Beeep!"

At the shrill whistle, I launched myself into the pool, a straight flat dive into the chlorine water. I was quickly into my stroke, pulling myself forward with my arms, kicking out my legs like a frog, as always loving the feel of pushing through the water. I stretched for the finish and touched with both hands. I thought I was first, and the timer for my lane soon confirmed it. But it hadn't been one of my best races. Although I'd won, it was the slowest heat. I'd need to do better to win that afternoon. Maybe my lunchtime drink would be just the pick-me-up I needed.

The heats carried on until a quarter past twelve when we broke for lunch. We were told to eat immediately in order to be ready to swim again at twenty past one. I sat with Joanna McAleese and Sharon Campbell, who'd qualified for the backstroke final. I'd intended to keep the contents of my beaker to myself, especially after the hockey débâcle, but when it came to it, I just had to tell them.

"Do you want to know what I've got in my beaker?"

"Looks like orange juice to me. So what?" Joanna said.

"Try it," I said.

She looked at the beaker suspiciously but took a sip anyway. Her face screwed up in disgust.

"Euch, what is it?"

I laughed. "Vodka and orange."

"You're not drinking that now, are you?" she said.

"Maybe," I answered.

"You'd better be careful," she said, but I could tell she was impressed.

I slugged it down, then settled to my fish-paste sandwiches and Tayto cheese and onion crisps. I could feel the alcohol slowly taking effect, smoothing the edges and helping me relax. I felt good.

Soon it was time for the afternoon races. As my event approached, I began to feel anxious. It was only just one hour since I'd had the vodka. What if you needed more than an hour with drink? What if it was dangerous? What if I got caught? There was no way Miss Park would let me away with drinking for a second time.

Suddenly I was desperate for the toilet. The final before mine was just about to start. Maybe I'd have time to get to the loo and back. I started towards the changing rooms.

Joanna McAleese grabbed my arm.

"Where are you going?"

"Toilet."

"There's no time. You'll miss the race."

"I've got to," I answered, breaking free of her grip.

Too late. The starter called us forward. I'd just have to hold on.

"Take your marks."

I got in position.

"Get set."

Instead of focusing my mind on winning, all I could think about was how quickly I could get to the toilet.

"Beeep!"

I was off, flying into the water. There was no time to lose. I needed to get to the toilet. I powered down the pool. The bar at the far end glistened before me. One last surge and I was touching it, climbing out and running past the timers, straight through to the changing rooms. The toilets were deserted, and I ripped down my costume and threw myself into the first cubicle, able to let go at last. Relief swept through me.

I sat in the toilet for a minute, letting my heart rate slow back down, then pulled up my wet costume, sliding my arms back through the holes. It was time to rejoin my team-mates. I tried to slip in discreetly, but Miss Park caught my eye. She beckoned me over.

"Where did you go? Are you all right?" she asked.

"Yes, fine," I answered. "I just really needed to go to the toilet."

She looked at me suspiciously but said nothing.

"Do you know where I came?" I asked.

"Don't you know?" she said.

"No. I went straight to the toilet. Did I beat Mary Anne McCabe?"

"Yes," she said. "And everyone else. You were first. Well done."

"Yes!" I said, a broad smile breaking out across my face.

Chapter 22

He's Not Coming Back

"Y OU KNOW YOUR father's going to England on Monday?"

"Aye," I grunted, barely looking up from the TV. I'd known for weeks that my father was going to Leeds to work for a year. This was old news.

"Well, he's not coming back."

It was a quarter to six on a Saturday evening, the day after Good Friday. I was watching *Jim'll Fix It* in the living room. My mum had arrived home in a strange white car a couple of minutes earlier. I'd thought it odd at the time; she usually got a lift with my dad on wet evenings like tonight.

I glanced out the window. The white car was still there. She followed my gaze.

"It's Tracy. She knows about me and your father. I'm going out with her and the girls to Bushmills tonight. I'll just go and get changed."

I heard her pounding up the stairs and thudding around the bedroom—she'd never been light on her feet. Ten minutes later she was back down, patting nervously at her skirt, checking her bag for keys and purse.

"You'll be OK, won't you." It was more a statement than a question.

I nodded.

"I might be back late. Don't wait up."

And with that she was off, out the door and down the driveway to the waiting white car. I watched Jeannette get out and open the door for her, squeezing her shoulder as my mother got in the car.

My sister came into the living room just as the white car reversed up and drove off. She'd arrived home with my mother, back from her Saturday job at Woolworth's. She'd been in the kitchen while my mum talked to me and appeared now with a doorstop corned-beef sandwich and a cup of tea.

"So, I suppose she's told you," she said with difficulty, mouth half full of corned beef and bread.

"Aye, how long've you known?"

"Since lunchtime—I popped into the shop at my break. Our Simon was there as well. So, what do you think?" she asked.

I had dreaded for some years that my parents would separate, ever since the Gilpins, who owned the bakery on Captain Street, had parted. Mr Gilpin had run off with some hussy who worked in the bookie's. It was the talk of the town. Their daughter, Janine, was in my sister's class. She'd never exactly been the life and soul. A dumpy, silent child beforehand, she withdrew even further, sitting quietly in the corner stuffing down crisps and chocolates and sweets while the other children went out to play. She became a figure of pity, talked about behind her back, rarely included.

It was bad having the town laughing stock as a father, but surely better than having no father at all? I shrugged and changed the subject.

"I suppose you're off out tonight?"

"Aye. To the Strand with Caroline."

"What about our Simon?"

"He was off drinking with Fenton and John McCall when I last seen him, so he'll probably be half slaughtered in Fairley's already. I think he was planning to go to Spudz to hear the X-Dreamysts tonight."

"What about my da? Do you know what he's up to? Is he going out?"

I was beginning to panic. My sister looked away.

"I think Mummy said he was starting to pack tonight. Anyway, I'm away to get changed." And with that, she scooted up the stairs and into the bathroom.

I looked out the window, realising why she'd moved so quickly. My father's car had just pulled into the driveway. He was making his way to the front door, a large suitcase in either hand.

I stared resolutely at the telly as he passed the living-room door and proceeded up the stairs with his cases. I heard him exchange a few words with Joanna and then the creak of floorboards above my head as he moved about my parents' bedroom.

The Generation Game finished and I decided I'd better get up and get on with making the tea. I was peeling potatoes for chips when my sister came back down, freshly washed, dressed and made up.

"Do I look all right?" she asked.

She wore spray-on red jeans and a black top, cut so low that everything was hanging out but the price ticket.

"You look great," I said.

"See you then," she said, pulling on her jacket.

I paused for a moment as I heard the front door shut behind her. Then I put the chip pan on and carried on peeling the potatoes. By the time they were washed and cut, the fat was nice and hot. It frothed and hissed as I lowered the chips into the pan.

Four pasties followed them. I loved pasties. Not the pastry kind you get in England. No, Irish pasties made of sausagemeat, onion and potato mashed together and formed into circles, half an inch thick, then dipped into batter and deep fried. Nothing tastier came out of a chip pan.

It didn't take long for the food to cook. I divided it between two plates and then went to the bottom of the stairs and shouted, "Dad, tea's ready."

There was no response.

"Dad!" I shouted, even louder. "Tea."

This time he heard.

"I'll be down in a minute."

I buttered a slice of white bread for a chip butty, lashed the smaller portion in vinegar, and took it into the living room to watch the TV.

I'd almost finished eating when my dad came down the stairs. He, too, brought his food into the living room, nodding briefly as he took a seat. We watched TV for a while, speaking not a word, exchanging not a glance. He finished his tea, put his plate on the floor and leaned back in his chair. He sat there for a few minutes before getting up and going back upstairs.

I gathered up our plates and took them through to the kitchen. I boiled the kettle and washed the dishes. Finally, I fed the dogs before retiring to the living room. My father continued to creak about upstairs. I remained firmly on the ground floor, watching the TV with the dogs.

I kept one wary eye on the living-room door, but it was

nine o'clock before he came back downstairs. He went into the kitchen. I'd barely had the chance to wonder what he was up to when he came into the living room and sat down in the chair opposite, sighing heavily.

We sat for a minute.

"Do you want a cup of tea?" I asked, to break the silence.

"Aye, that'd be nice."

I retreated to the kitchen and put the kettle on to boil and two slices of plain bread under the grill. When the toast was done, I applied a thick coating of Golden Cow butter and put it on a plate along with a round of my mother's short-bread and a coconut haystack. I poured the tea into his Silver Jubilee mug and took it and the plate into the living room.

"Ta," he said.

The news had finished and the opening bars of *Starsky and Hutch* were just sounding. I sat back down in my chair.

"Do you mind if I watch this?" I asked him.

He said nothing and I wasn't sure if he'd heard me.

"*Starsky and Hutch?*" I said. "Do you mind if I watch it?"

"What?" he said. "No, no. Go ahead. I'm going to have a bath in a minute. As soon as the water's had a chance to warm up."

I tried to settle into *Starsky and Hutch* but it was difficult. We sat silently.

"I'm away to run my bath," he said eventually, and departed upstairs.

He was gone for some time. I was ensconced in *Match of the Day* when he returned in pyjamas, dressing-gown and slippers.

"Who's playing?" he asked.

"Spurs and Liverpool."

He stood watching it for a moment and then turned back to me.

"I heard the results earlier. I think I'll just get off to bed," he said.

My relief was premature. He didn't go. Instead he hovered in the doorway. I waited for him to say something. But nothing came. Eventually he turned away.

"Good night," he said, over his shoulder.

"Night," I said.

I watched the rest of *Match of the Day*, then took the dogs out for their late-night walk. It was quiet as we made our way up the Ballycairn Road to the post box and back.

I made some toast and hot Ribena when I got back home to enjoy with the late-night movie. I'd missed the first half an hour of *The Mummy*, but the plot wasn't hard to pick up. I'd seen it before anyway, shuffling across the screen, one arm held stiffly out before it.

About one in the morning, a car drew up outside the door. It stayed there, engine running, for an eternity. My mother never could get straight out of a car. Then a door slammed, and a minute later I heard her struggling to get her key in the lock. I got up and opened the door.

"Hello, love," she said in a stage whisper. "Are you still up?"

She swayed slightly as she followed me into the living room and collapsed into an armchair. She lay there for a minute, eyes closed, breathing heavily. I thought she'd fallen asleep, but then she rocked her head forward and opened her eyes.

"Where's your da?"

"He went to bed ages ago. In your room."

She rolled her eyes. "Bastard!"

"Do you want anything? Tea? Toast?"

"No, just a glass of water."

I went and got the water, running the tap till it was good and cold.

Her eyes were shut again when I returned, and I shook her gently to wake her. She smelt of drink and cigarettes.

"Here you are, Mummy."

"Thanks, love. You're a great girl. I don't know what I'd do without you."

She was just finishing her water when Joanna and Simon arrived home. They'd got a lift from one of Joanna's friends. Simon staggered into the living room and threw himself down on the sofa. Twelve hours of solid drinking had taken their toll.

"Are you all right, son?" My mother's voice was full of concern.

"Mmmm." He grunted but didn't move.

"I think we should all get to bed," Joanna said. She disappeared off up the stairs.

My mother and I got to our feet. I didn't know how she could face sleeping with my father in the circumstances. Simon refused to move from the sofa. In the end, I fetched a sleeping bag and draped it over him.

"Good night," I said, and went to bed.

Despite the late night, I woke early the next morning. I slipped downstairs for some digestives, then retreated back to bed to read.

At about nine o'clock there was a light knock on the door.

"Constance, Joanna, are you awake?" It was my mum's voice.

"Yeah," I answered. "I am anyway."

Joanna groaned in protest. My mother's head appeared round the door.

"You need to get up. Your dad's decided to leave today. He's just getting washed and having his breakfast and then he'll be off."

I forced myself out of bed and shrugged on jeans and a T-shirt. But Joanna lay on.

"Are you not getting up?" I asked.

"I'll be down soon," she answered, yawning.

I left her to it and went downstairs. I found my mother in the kitchen, frying sausages and bacon in one pan, scrambling eggs in another. Of my father, there was no sign.

"Where is he?" I whispered.

"Getting dressed," she answered. "He'll be down in a minute."

"What about Simon? Is he still on the sofa?"

"No, he must have got up in the night and gone to bed. I've already woken him; he'll be down soon."

I helped my mother finish the breakfast: removing the sausages and bacon from the pan to a Pyrex plate and putting them in the oven to stay warm, then frying potato bread and soda farls in the bacon fat. My mother put on the kettle for the inevitable tea while I laid the table, putting out salt, butter, red and brown ketchup.

My father appeared first, Old Spice clouding the air around him. He nodded to me by way of greeting and sat down at the table.

The lid of the kettle rattled a couple of times and then it began to whistle, hesitantly at first but developing into a solid complaint. I took it from the heat, tossed some tea into the pot, poured on the boiling water and put the tea on the stove to draw.

My mother went to the bottom of the stairs.

"Joanna! Simon!" she called. "Your breakfast's ready."

Then she returned to the kitchen and started serving out the scrambled eggs.

Joanna came first, wrapped up in her peach dressing-gown. Then Simon. He looked hellish, face fawn, eyes blood-shot.

Soon we were all sitting round the table, eating cooked breakfast. There wasn't much conversation. In fact, only the scraping of knives and forks on plates and the occasional request for the butter or ketchup covered the silence.

I ate quickly, wanting to escape. But when it came to it, it felt too difficult to excuse myself and leave the table, too brutal to reject my father in his last minutes at home with us.

My dad was last to finish, lingering over the final few slices of bacon. We sat waiting for him to make a move. At last he pushed his chair back from the table.

"There's nothing to beat a cooked breakfast," he said, before standing up and going upstairs.

I heard the toilet flush, then the bumping and banging of my father dragging the two big suitcases down the stairs and out to the car.

I sat tense in my chair. How was I supposed to say goodbye? Would I have to kiss him? That's what I did when I said goodbye to my grandparents. I flinched at the idea. I couldn't remember ever having kissed him and didn't want to start now. Maybe a handshake, I thought, but dismissed it almost immediately—too formal. Would he expect tears? I'd none to shed, not for now anyway.

I'd decided on "I'll see you soon" when Joanna broke the silence.

"What's he up to? What's he doing out there?"

"God knows," my mother replied. "You know what he's like for going off on an expedition."

"I can't stand just sitting here waiting," Joanna said.

I knew how she felt. I wanted it over. If he was going, let him get on with it.

"One of us should go and see what he's up to," I said.

No one spoke. It was down to me.

"Do you want me to go?" I said.

"Would you, love? Thanks."

I crept through to the living room, half crouching as if that would stop him seeing me. I needn't have bothered. He wasn't out there. Neither was the car. He'd already gone.

Chapter 23

Three Visits

I SAW MY father only three more times. The first of these was a Sunday morning, two weeks after he left. I was dreading his arrival. My sister and I had received a short but gushing letter a few days after his departure. Written on hotel notepaper, it opened: "My darling angels".

For as long as I could remember, he'd referred to me with one insult or another. Pasty face, gormless, yokel or half-wit. He'd often string them together in a stream of abuse: "Look at you, you gormless half-wit. It's no wonder you're so pasty faced, when all you eat is toast and cream crackers."

The letter continued:

I miss you so much it's like my arm has been cut off. You have always been the centre of my life and will always remain so.

I'm writing to you from a hotel in Leeds where I'm staying until I get somewhere permanent to live. Then you'll be welcome to visit me. I will visit you as often as I can.

And I will carry on supporting you, as I have always done.

Look after yourselves, my princesses, until I see you again.

Love, Dad

The letter made me nervous. I didn't know what to expect next.

He pulled into the driveway about eleven in the morning. I'd abandoned church by then and was sitting in the living room doing my physics homework.

"Mummy, he's here," I shouted up the stairs.

"Well, let him in," she called back. "I'll be down in a minute."

I went to the door and opened it, though he still had a key and my mum hadn't changed the locks. But my dad wasn't there. I peered out. Still no sign. Maybe he was in the car. But then I heard the faint rumble of the trailer as he hauled it from the side garden to the front of the house. He'd not taken it with him when he'd left two weeks before. Satisfied himself with the two huge suitcases then. But today was obviously going to be the big clear out. Maybe he'd found somewhere to live.

He nodded briefly when he saw me.

"Where's your mother?"

"She's just coming. I'll put the kettle on."

He followed me into the kitchen where my mother joined us. "How was your journey?" she asked.

"Not bad," he said. "I stayed at Gertrude's last night. Drove down this morning."

I made the tea.

"Do you want some breakfast?" my mum said.

Always the good Irish hostess, my mother. Never let anyone across your threshold without offering them food.

"I'd breakfast at Gertrude's," he said, "but I'd not say no to some shortbread if you've got any."

I brought his tea and shortbread over to the table.

"Where's Joanna?" he said.

"She's just getting dressed," my mother replied. "She'll be down in a minute."

"And Simon?"

"He went back to university last week."

"Oh. Of course."

The conversation dried up after that.

"Well, I'd better get started," he said eventually.

"I've moved all your things into the lounge ready for packing," my mother said.

We'd done it together, the night before. We found all sorts of things in his wardrobe in the landing. Shoes. Boxes and boxes of shoes. The whole bottom of the wardrobe was covered with boxes of brand-new shoes. Twelve pairs in total.

"What in the name of God did he want with all these shoes?" my mother said as we brought them down and laid them out in the lounge. There were loafers and brogues and ankle boots and trainers in black and brown and beige and white.

"And where did he get the money for them?"

There were new shirts as well, some still in their cellophane wrappers, others hanging up. And new jeans and trousers and a navy waterproof jacket.

"God, it's no wonder he never wanted anyone looking in this wardrobe," she said.

My dad also had a wardrobe in my parents' bedroom, but it was the one on the landing that agitated him. It had two doors with a narrow mirror between them. If he caught you looking at yourself, he'd say, "Get away from my wardrobe. If I catch you near that wardrobe again I'll swing for you."

One evening the year before, when I'd been at home on my own, I'd opened it carefully and looked inside. It didn't have all the new clothes then, but there was a huge box of condoms in packs of three. I took one with me to school to show my best friend, Alyson. We were repelled and thrilled at the same time.

She asked me where I'd got them. I lied, told her I'd found them near the Inst. playing fields. I didn't want her to know that they were my father's, didn't want to know myself.

We tried flushing one down the toilet. But it didn't go first time. We were panic-stricken, waiting anxiously for the cistern to fill so we could try again. We had better luck the second time but decided not to push it. We wrapped the remaining two in some tissues and stuffed them far down in one of the bins. Then we ran away from the toilets, laughing madly.

As we ferried his new clothes downstairs, my mum got more and more angry.

"D'you see all the things that bastard has got for himself? I've not even a decent pair of knickers to call my own. I know he's your father, but he's one rotten bastard from hell. He'd no time to be buying anything for any of youse, but by God he didn't stint when it came to himself.

"When I think what he's put me through, scrimping and scraping to make ends meet. Taking in knitting jobs that pay a halfpenny. Selling all your clothes on to the thrift shop to help buy the next things youse needed. Planning every single penny that that mean bastard gave me to put food on the table. And meanwhile he's out spending money like a man with no arms. Your granda's right. He is a low-down, selfish, hateful piece of dirt. May God forgive me for saying so, but it's no word of a lie."

I think she enjoyed her moment of defiance that Sunday morning as she flaunted the fact that she'd been through his precious wardrobe. She'd seen his secret stash. She'd also made a list of everything we'd found, thinking it would come in handy when it came to the court case and sorting out maintenance. Maybe my father came to the same conclusion, as he increased the monthly allowance he was sending from £40 to £50. Said that he recognised that she'd need some help sorting herself out and that even though he was no longer at home so she'd not need as much food, still he wanted to do what was best.

But he had to dig deeper still when the case came to court: my mother was awarded £160 per month. My dad transferred the bills into her name, but she was still quids in compared to when he'd been living there.

We left him to pack the trailer on his own. My mother and I began preparing the Sunday lunch, me peeling potatoes, while she rubbed butter into the flesh of a chicken, ready for roasting, trying to ignore his trips back and forth, back and forth. My sister sat at the table, telling us about who'd been dancing with who at the Strand disco the night before.

It felt like his trips would never end, but eventually they did. He came into the kitchen. "Well, I think I'm done," he said.

No one answered.

"So I suppose I'd better be off then."

My mother nodded.

Suddenly his eyes were wet, and then he started to sob,

leaning against the kitchen sink for support. I sat appalled, not knowing what to say or do. I'd never seen him cry before. My sister, too, sat mute. After what felt like two hours but can have been only a couple of minutes, my mother said, "Come on now, Victor. This doesn't do anybody any good." She passed him a tissue.

He wiped his eyes and blew his nose. "Sorry," he said. Another first. "I'd best go. Gertrude's expecting me. I'll see you in a few weeks, girls."

Moments later he was driving away, bulging trailer following behind.

My mother and I set about finishing the preparation of our Sunday dinner. I mashed the potatoes while she boiled the carrots and peas. We were both focused on our tasks, but I could feel the storm brewing behind me.

"Is dinner still not ready?" my sister said as my mother started making bread sauce from a packet mix.

"It'll only be a few minutes now," my mother said, trying for calm but sounding fake.

"Jesus, it's always the same in this house. Nothing's ever done on time. Waiting ages to eat some rotten muck."

My mother said nothing. Neither did I.

"God, it's no wonder he left."

I turned and gave Joanna a warning look.

"And you can shove it, too," she said to me. "Miss Goody Two Shoes. My daddy was right. Mummy always preferred you and Simon. Well, you just stick together, why don't you? I'm going to go and live with my daddy, and then the two of you can sit here shoving that rubbish down your throats in peace. I know when I'm not wanted."

My mother spoke at last.

"Of course you're wanted. I want you. And so does Constance. Don't you?"

"Yes," I said, but with little conviction.

"Not as much as my daddy. My daddy loves me. Not like you. You don't love me. You don't want me. But he does. He wants me. He told me he wanted me to come with him. Not her," she said, pointing at me. "Just me. He wants me to come, and I'm going. I'm going to England to be with him."

"Oh, Joanna, have some sense," my mother said. "He doesn't love you. He's never loved anyone but himself. This is where your…" But before she'd finished her sentence my sister had picked up the empty plate in front of her and smashed it on the ground.

"I hate you," she screamed. "I fucking hate you."

She ran from the kitchen, slamming the door behind her. My mother went after her. I heard the front door clash shut and my mother shouting, "Joanna, Joanna. Come back." But she didn't. Not till that evening. She went straight upstairs.

"Should I go and talk to her?" my mum asked.

"No, just leave her for now."

My mother waited a minute, then went to the bottom of the stairs.

"Joanna," she shouted. "Is that you?"

There was no reply. My mother came back in.

"Will you go and talk to her?" she said to me.

"Just leave her to come down. She'll come if she wants."

My mother wasn't convinced, but a few minutes later Joanna came and joined us. We didn't talk about my dad's visit, what had happened, where she'd been. We watched Sunday-night TV instead, but all night my father hovered around the room.

A few days later, another of his letters arrived. It set my
sister off on a fresh wave of wanting to go and live with him:
how she hated me and my mum, how I was the favourite
because I did well at school, how nobody cared about her
but my dad, how he'd been the only one to show any interest in her education.

She seemed to have forgotten the days of the parent
governor meetings, the clipboards and questioning, the
review she couldn't take, the art he made her drop.

That evening, he phoned to say he'd be over the following week. My sister arranged for him to pick her up first
and then come to collect me when my school finished at
3.30 p.m.

I didn't want to be picked up outside school; didn't want
everyone seeing us meeting him. The thing I'd always
dreaded about my parents splitting up was what people
would think. Nearly everyone I knew had parents who were
firmly together. Anyone else without a father, it was because
he'd died. I wished that mine had, too. I didn't want everyone whispering about me as they had with Janine Gilpin.

I was dreading the end of school the day of his visit, but
the beginning wasn't great either. As I arrived at the school
gates, I bumped into Megan and Julie, two friends from the
junior netball team. I'd not seen much of them since before
Easter, when the netball season finished.

"Hiya," Julie said, as they fell into stride beside me.

"Hi," I answered.

"I wanted to ask you something," Julie said. "You know
your dad's away in England?"

I nodded, anxiety flickering. Julie's father worked for the
same company as my dad. What did she know?

"Isn't it that he's just working there for a year? Megan says that your parents have split up, but she's got it wrong, hasn't she?"

Oh God! I'd told only two people about the break-up: Alyson and Miss Park. I didn't want to talk about it to anyone else. I knew people would get to know—like all small towns, Coleraine loved to gossip—but why did they have to mention it to me?

"No," I said eventually. "Megan's right."

The shock on Julie's face was plain.

"Oh," she said. "Sorry."

I drifted through the first part of the day—assembly and then double French. But things picked up during my third lesson, PE with Miss Park. I loved PE—shimmying up ropes, vaulting boxes, whacking hockey balls. At the end of the lesson, Miss Park called Alyson and me into her office.

"How would you two like this afternoon off classes to help me out at the Milk Cup heats?"

The Milk Cup was an athletics competition for first years. Alyson and I had competed the year before. We'd even got our picture in the local paper as winners of the Coleraine and District heats.

"Oh, yes, please," Alyson said. "What do you want us to do?"

"You'll be helping me measure in the long jump and giving our girls a bit of encouragement. We're setting off at ten to one. I'll sort it out with your teachers."

The heats were held at the Inst.'s athletics track, near my house. We got a lift in Miss Park's bright green Ford Escort. The first event was the girls' 100 metres, which Alyson had won the previous year. Our runner, Cathy Conway, managed fourth. Then it was the 200 metres, 800 metres, long jump and shot put before the relay finale.

By a quarter to four, the competition was over. The Coleraine High School team was placed third in the girls' competition, not quite good enough to qualify for the semi-finals.

"Thanks for your help," Miss Park said to me. "You've not far to go home now."

I looked away and nodded. Miss Park was my favourite teacher, and I was normally very chatty. "Is something wrong?" she asked.

"Oh, no," I said.

"Are you sure? You're acting a bit strange."

"Well, it's just that I'm not going home. I've got to go back to school. I'm meeting my father there."

"What time are you meeting him?"

"Half past three," I muttered.

"Half three! Well what are you doing here? You should have told me this earlier. I would have got someone else to help."

"I didn't want you to get someone else. I'd rather be here than meeting him."

"Oh, Constance, whatever he's done, he's still your father. Come on. I'll give you a lift."

"But it's not on your way home."

I knew exactly where Miss Park lived and the route from here to there. On a Sunday, I'd often walk the dogs out past her house, three miles away.

"Oh, it's not that far out of my way," she said. "Come on."

I followed as she strode quickly to her car. Five minutes later we were pulling up outside the High School. It was four o'clock and I was half an hour late. I got out, looking around for my father's blue car, hoping they'd gone without me. But it was still there, waiting just beyond the main entrance. I forced myself to walk towards it. I opened the back door and got in, expecting a tirade. But instead he said, "Oh, darling, here you are at last. We were beginning to worry about you."

The reason he was being so nice was staring me in the face.

"Constance, this is Irene. Irene, this is Constance, my youngest daughter."

Irene smiled. "Hello, it's nice to meet you at last. Your father's told me so much about you."

I grunted hello, the minimum level of manners I thought I could get away with.

Irene! I couldn't believe he'd brought Irene! The woman he'd been having an affair with for the past three years. The woman my father had sworn didn't exist, right up until the weekend he left, when my mother confronted him with receipts for hotels and gifts she'd found amongst his clothes.

What was he doing bringing her? And on his first proper visit. And what was she doing coming? Wanting to get her feet under our table.

We drove the four miles to Portstewart. The radio was on so I didn't have to talk. We found a parking space on the prom, where we'd parked so often as a family. Ahead of us the Atlantic sparkled, and it was clear enough to see Donegal.

We got out of the car and crossed the road to the shop side of the prom. My father linked his arm with Irene's as they window-shopped their way along to the Stewart Hotel where he'd decided to take us for tea. I trailed along behind, head down, praying no one would see us. I was furious.

How dare he parade his strumpet to the world as if they'[...] done nothing wrong? And just turning up with her with n[...] warning, assuming we'd want to meet her? Making a show [...] us along Portstewart's main street?

We passed Morelli's, a glass-fronted ice-cream parlou[...] popular with my school friends. I didn't dare look in, in cas[...] someone saw me.

Thank God we're not going there, I thought. *At least in th[...] Stewart we can't be seen from the road.*

I decided that the sooner we got there, the better, and pu[...] a spurt on, so I was now ahead of my father, his mistress an[...] my sister. A minute later, I was in the lobby of the hotel. It wa[...] a holidaymakers' hotel, still fairly quiet at this time of year. I[...] would be really bad luck if someone we knew was there. [...] heard the swish of the revolving door behind me and turne[...] to see my father, Irene and Joanna emerge.

It was only 4.30 and the dining room was almost empty[...] only an elderly couple lingering over the last fragments o[...] their afternoon tea. A dozen tables were set, ready for th[...] main evening sitting between five and seven. We were show[...] to one of them, taking our places round the four sides. A[...] minute later the waitress returned with four menus.

I buried my head in my menu, ignoring the stiff conver[...] sation of the others. I took plenty of time to weigh up the[...] available options:

Soup of the day
Orange juice
Prawn cocktail
Melon
. . . .

Gammon and pineapple
Chicken Maryland
Roast beef
Battered haddock
All served with a selection of vegetables and potatoes

Prawn cocktail was a simple choice for starter, but I struggled for a while between gammon and chicken Maryland. Eventually the gammon won out. I carried on perusing the menu, avoiding eye contact to stave off the moment when I'd have to engage with my father and the dreaded Irene.

But then I felt my sister nudge me, quite hard.

"Constance," she said, "Irene's talking to you."

I looked up from my menu at last to meet Irene's gaze, her muddy eyes staring into mine. She smiled, but it stayed strictly at lip level. Her face was hard. This was a very different woman from my mother.

"I was just saying that you're a quiet one."

I held her gaze, defiant for a moment, and then answered, "Mmmm."

"Oh, she's always been quiet," my father said. "Always the quiet one, our Constance. Isn't that right?"

He looked towards me, expecting me to affirm. But I was boiling again. What did he know? What did he know about what I was like? He was never there. And when he was, he wasn't interested. The quiet one—they'd have laughed at school if I'd told them. I'd been voted form rep., form captain and hockey team captain. That wasn't from being the quiet one. He knew nothing about me.

Anger was an unfamiliar feeling around my father. A welcome alternative to fear. It made me giddy, bold about my behaviour.

But the waitress arrived at that moment, and the attention switched from me to ordering the food. I despised Irene's choice of orange juice and roast beef, delighted that she was not going for anything I was having.

A smattering of guests had been arriving while I'd been locked behind the menu. I looked around furtively and was relieved to find no one I recognised.

I made brief responses to their continuing attempts to engage me in conversation while we waited for our food:

My father: "How's school going?"

Me: "OK."

Irene: "What's your favourite subject?"

Me: "None in particular."

My father: "Have your exams started yet?"

Me: "No."

My sister interjected at this point. "Mine start next week. I'm doing my CSEs," she explained to Irene. They discussed the subjects she was taking and the timetable of exams.

And then the food arrived. My father ordered a second round of drinks: gin and tonics for him and Irene, Coke for my sister, Club Orange for me. The whiff of gin reminded me of my terrible hangover from a few months before. I turned my head away, slightly nauseated, and focused on my prawn cocktail.

We'd barely finished when the second course arrived. I helped make space on the table for boiled potatoes, chips, carrots and peas. And as I moved things around, I "accidentally" managed to knock my almost full glass in the direction of Irene.

A flood of orange swept towards her, but she was quick for a large woman and headed it off with a napkin while getting to her feet. The damage was limited. She couldn't prove it was deliberate, but I'm sure she knew. I was glad. I wanted her to know. She'd never win me round, so she might as well leave me alone.

After we'd eaten, we walked back to the car. Joanna and I walked ahead.

"Don't mention Irene to Mummy," she said. "It'll only upset her."

I knew this was true.

"Won't she see her when he drops us off?"

"No, I've already asked him to stop at the top of the road. Said I've got to pop in to see one of my friends."

I nodded. "OK."

The journey home was quick. There were tears in his eyes again as we kissed him on the cheek and said goodbye.

I didn't hear from him for ages after that, though he still phoned my sister quite often. Her loyalties remained divided, even after he refused to contribute to her upbringing when the maintenance case finally came to court.

My birthday came and went without even a card, let alone a present.

And then, a couple of weeks before Christmas, a card arrived containing £21 to be divided equally between my brother, sister and me. A short note informed us that he'd be in Ireland that weekend and would like to take us out for lunch. It gave a number where he could be contacted. Joanna sorted out the arrangements—he'd be picking us up at half eleven on Saturday.

My mother set off for work as usual about half eight. Although it was the first day of my holidays, I was up before she left. About an hour later, my brother surfaced. He'd arrived home from university the evening before.

"What time's he coming?" he asked.

"My da? About half eleven."

"I don't know how you can bear to see him," he said. "Bastard."

I shrugged. I wasn't aware of having any choice.

"Well, I'm not sticking around," he said. "I'm off out in half an hour. But since I'm not going to be here, I need you to do something for me. Give him back my share of the £21. I don't want it. And you can tell him that from me."

He handed me an envelope. Inside were a fiver and two pound notes.

I'd not been looking forward to seeing my father, but full-scale dread now descended upon me. It was going to be awful giving back the money. I should have said no, but Simon was another person in my life who I found it hard to say no to, so I took the envelope and nodded.

True to his word, Simon was off thirty minutes later. At half ten I woke Joanna and left her to get herself ready while I returned to the TV in the living room with the dogs.

My father arrived on time. We drove down towards the town centre and the free car park just before the Old Bridge. It was a cold day, and he put on a sheepskin coat and scarf hat and gloves in assorted tartans. It seemed his Scottish phase still wasn't over, though at least he'd dropped the accent. I had on a long olive mohair coat with threads of gold and red that I'd bought second-hand in Oxfam, over a black mohair jumper and black jodhpurs. I'd finished off with black Doc Marten boots. My sister was the most normal in jeans, a jumper and a winter coat from Dunnes.

We walked across the bridge and on into Bridge Street.

Ahead lay the Diamond and Coleraine's main shopping street, certain to be full of people out buying Christmas presents. We were bound to meet someone; it was just a question of who. I was just steeling myself when I heard my dad say, "This is new."

He was referring to Café Delish, which had recently opened on Bridge Street. I'd not been there myself but was delighted when he suggested we go in. I steered us away from the draught of the door to a seat where we wouldn't be seen. Our order was taken quickly, and it wasn't long before I was getting stuck into battered sausage, chips and beans.

It was as well that the service was so speedy as we were running out of things to say after five minutes. Eating helped to cover the gaps in our conversation, and we gladly ordered Christmas pudding with cream for afters. By the end of lunch, we'd covered how I was getting on at school, how cold it was, what Joanna thought of the technical college, how we preferred it cold to wet, how good the food was, and what prospects there were for snow. We avoided his new life in England without us and our new life in Coleraine without him, and if ever the conversation edged in a direction that might cause them to be mentioned—such as whether we'd done all our Christmas shopping and how long the tree had been up—we'd veer back towards safer territory.

We didn't linger after finishing the pudding.

"Well, I suppose we'd best be off," he said. "I'm sure you've both got things to do, and I've got to be in Belfast for half two."

We got back into our outdoor coverings.

"What are you going to do now?" I asked Joanna as we waited outside the café while my dad paid the bill.

"I'm meeting Brendan and Janice in Woollie's, then fi
ishing my shopping," she said. "What about you?"

"I've got to pop into Hamilton's wool shop. Then I mig
go home." This was a lie, but I didn't want to give Simor
money back in front of Joanna. Hamilton's lay back acro
the bridge, away from the main shopping centre, near whe
the car was parked.

My dad appeared, muffled up behind his array of tarta

My sister put her arms round him briefly.

"Thanks for lunch," she said. "Have a nice Christmas."

"Thanks, love."

She set off up Bridge Street. He turned to me.

"I'll walk back with you over the bridge," I said. "I've g
to do a message at Hamilton's."

He nodded.

It was a short walk. I needed to get on with the dirty dee
but I still couldn't face it. We were approaching the turn o
to the car park when I finally blurted out, "These are fo
you."

I handed him a sealed envelope containing a Christma
card that I'd written to him:

> To Dad
> Merry Christmas and a Happy New Year
> Love, Constance

and the one Simon had given me containing his share of th
money.

Before he'd time to open them, I blundered on, "Th
card's from me. The other's from Simon. He said he didn
want it."

There was a pause as he peered into the unsealed env

lope and saw the money. Even though I'd told him what it meant, it took a minute before it registered. Tears flashed behind his eyes. He nodded but didn't speak.

"I'm sorry," I said.

He nodded again, looking away, down the river.

I gave him an awkward hug.

"See you next time," I said and walked off to Hamilton's without looking back.

But there never was a next time. It was the last time I ever saw him.

He didn't die; he just didn't bother. He didn't visit, didn't call, didn't write. The only sign that he remembered my existence came almost two years later on my sixteenth birthday. He didn't send a card. No. He sent a letter. To my mother. Explaining that now I was "of age" it was no longer his responsibility to support me. She had to go to court to get the maintenance reinstated.

Another two years passed, and on my eighteenth birthday he tried the same stunt. As I was in my final year of school, the judge ordered him to carry on paying.

Still, at least he hadn't forgotten me.

By contrast I did everything I could to forget him. Forget him and everything about him. But then I've always been a little forgetful. Always had a lot to forget.

Ridley Beeton

FACETS OF OLIVE SCHREINER

A Manuscript Source-book

Olive Schreiner always had an effect on people – no-one who encountered her was afterwards neutral about her. She was adored or thoroughly loathed. In this collection of letters, diaries and other manuscript sources, Ridley Beeton integrates her warmth and arrogance, her anger and love, her brilliance and contrariness into a comprehensive portrait of Olive Schreiner the woman and writer. The emotional/intellectual entanglements with Karl Pearson, Edward Carpenter and Havelock Ellis are extensively covered. The facts presented are based on primary sources held at research centres, and are linked by notes which give further information about the people who influenced her, or under whose guidance she worked.

275 pages, a paperbook

Janet Hodgson

PRINCESS EMMA

The gracious oaks of Bishopscourt, Cape Town, sheltered the
first private school intended to provide a black elite which would
civilise the intransigent tribes of the Eastern Frontier.

At least, this was the fervent hope of Bishop Robert Gray
and his colonial colleague, governor Sir George Grey, when
they collaborated in founding Zonnebloem College 'for the
education of the sons (and daughters) of chiefs.' Emma, daughter
of Xhosa chieftain Sandile, was among the first of these children
to be snatched from the jaws of heathenism and introduced
to the advantages of western education. The results of this
conflict between the traditional and the new 'European' culture,
were often unfortunate and tragic. Emma's story vividly
describes the extent of the dilemma, and the implications for
the hundreds of thousands of her nation, as a direct consequence
of the experiment. This book provides an entirely new
perspective of the evolution of Xhosa society in the wake of
this colonial experiment.

200 pages, a paperbook